The Unknown Islands

NOTES AND LANDSCAPES

BELLIS AZORICA SERIES

SERIES EDITORS:
Onésimo T. Almeida & Mario Pereira

EDITORIAL BOARD:
Diniz Borges
Maria do Rosário Girão
Urbano Bettencourt
Vamberto Freitas
Victor Rui Dores

Vitorino Nemésio, *Stormy Isles: An Azorean Tale*
Translated and introduced by Francisco Cota Fagundes

Pedro da Silveira, *Poems in Absentia* &
Poems from *The Island and the World*
Translated by George Monteiro
Foreword by Vamberto Freitas
Afterword by George Monteiro

Adelaide Freitas, *Smiling in the Darkness*
Translated by Katharine F. Baker, Bobby J. Chamberlain,
Reinaldo F. Silva, and Emanuel Mel
Foreword by João de Melo

Raul Brandão, *The Unknown Islands*
Translated by David Brookshaw
Introduction by Urbano Bettencourt

Natália Correia, *In America, I Discovered I Was European*
Translated by Katharine F. Baker and Emanuel Melo
Introduction by Onésimo T. Almeida

The Unknown Islands

NOTES AND LANDSCAPES

Raul Brandão

◇◇◇

TRANSLATED BY DAVID BROOKSHAW

INTRODUCTION BY URBANO BETTENCOURT

TAGUS PRESS
University of Massachusetts Dartmouth
Dartmouth, MA

*Tagus Press is the publishing arm of the
Center for Portuguese Studies and Culture at
the University of Massachusetts Dartmouth.*
Center director: Victor K. Mendes

Bellis Azorica 4
Tagus Press at the University of Massachusetts Dartmouth
Original Portuguese text © 1926 Raul Brandão
Translation © 2020 David Brookshaw
Introductionn © 2020 Urbano Bettencourt

All rights reserved
Manufactured in the United States of America

 GOVERNO
DOS **AÇORES**
This book was published with the support of
the Government of the Azores.

 REPÚBLICA
PORTUGUESA
CULTURA
DIREÇÃO-GERAL DO LIVRO, DOS ARQUIVOS E
DAS BIBLIOTECAS
This work was supported, in part, by the
Direção-Geral do Livro, dos Arquivos e das
Bibliotecas/Portugal (DGLAB)

Executive editor: Mario Pereira
Series editors: Onésimo T. Almeida & Mario Pereira
Copyedited by Dawn Potter
Designed and typeset by Jen Jackowitz

For all inquiries, please contact
Tagus Press
Center for Portuguese Studies and Culture
University of Massachusetts Dartmouth
285 Old Westport Road
North Dartmouth, MA 02747–2300
(508) 999-8255, fax (508) 999-9272
https://www.umassd.edu/portuguese-studies-center/

ISBN: 978-1-951470-00-5
Library of Congress control number: 2020937954

TO MY FRIENDS IN THE AZORES

Contents

◇◇◇

Raul Brandão in the Azores

BETWEEN WONDER AND ENCHANTMENT

In the summer of 1924, Raul Brandão spent two months on a visit to the Azores. He recorded his memory of that sojourn in *The Unknown Islands* (1926), a book that also discusses Madeira, because Brandão's trip to the Azores included passage through that other archipelago. At the time of his visit, Brandão was one of Portugal's most respected writers, and his reputation had been enhanced during the previous year with the publication and successful reception of *Os Pescadores* (The Fishermen, 1923), which was likewise the product of travel, this time along the coast of continental Portugal. In that book, Brandão combined his distinctive and self-assured writing style with impressionistic descriptions of landscape as well as incisive and profound portraits of figures whose suffering and humility had prompted him to reflect on time, life, and death. After the success of *Os Pescadores*, readers who learned of the writer's upcoming travels to the Azores had high expectations for what *The Unknown Islands* would become: a great work of Portuguese travel literature. It is certainly, as the poet and researcher Pedro da Silveira

affirmed, the best book about the Azores written by someone not from the archipelago.

The islands have undergone many changes in the inter-
vening decades, such as an improved standard of living, more
extensive interisland relations, and expanded contact with
the world. Yet today *The Unknown Islands* maintains its capacity to surprise and captivate us. What explains the durability
of (to use the author's own words) this "interview with the
Azores"? Why does it makes us feel like the contemporaries
of the people we meet in it? How does it allow us to experience their abandonment, their solitude? Certainly, Brandão's
work reaches far beyond the limits of its modest subtitle—
Notes and Landscapes. Rather than simply recording what
appears on the surface and taking notes on the landscape
of the islands as a simple, hurried traveler and collector of
impressions might, Brandão went to the Azores to discover a
land and to understand its people in their relation to the the
space around them.

His trip was, he said, the realization of "an old idea." In an
interview he gave shortly after his return from the Azores, he
said that the visit had been planned for many years. Curiosity
about Corvo had been his main impetus. As Vasco Medeiros
Rosa has recently revealed, Brandão had written an article
on Corvo in 1909, many years before his journey to the archipelago, which remained unpublished.[1] In that article, he celebrated the island's communitarian lifestyle and grassroots
approach to social organization, which emphasized harmony
and reduced conflicts. "Corvo is a Christian democracy
made up of farmers," he would later write in *The Unknown
Islands*, which, in some respects, is a comparison of observed

---

[1] See Vasco Medeiros Rosa, *Raul Brandão e os Açores* (Lajes do Pico: Com-
panhia das Ilhas, 2019).

reality and the secondhand information he had received and reported in his earlier, unpublished article.

This was a voyage that had been previously planned (and this can be seen from information in the book that was not the product of his direct observation) with a fundamental purpose. Given his preexisting interest in Corvo, Brandão decided to begin his "discovery" of the Azores with that island. Yet even en route from Lisbon, he took the opportunity to learn and observe. The boat's gradual approach to the archipelago provided moments of revelation and wonder that superimposed the immediate present onto two notions of deep time: he imagined the volcanic islands, finally formed, resting on the surface of the waters on the first day of their existence and he imagined them emerging from the sea, mysterious to the eyes of the historical discoverer. This helps us understand the first vision that Brandão offers us of the landscape of São Jorge, perceived as gigantic and intimidating, and for this reason he expressed terror and awe at the vision of this formidable landscape that inspires awareness of the insignificance of man.

It is on Corvo that Brandão experiences the shock of encountering the Other (in this case, the Azorean) and it is here on the smallest island of the archipelago that he begins his slow and patient journey through the islands, moving from west to east in the direction of his return route to continental Portugal. From a symbolic point of view, it is on Corvo that this twentieth-century "discoverer" finally sets foot on land after having traversed the seas in order to approach the people, to come into contact with them, to confront a world that is foreign to him for diverse reasons, a amazement that would become bewilderment and anguish. Later, back home in Lisbon, he confessed, "It makes me want to cry when I recall the affection and tenderness with which they treated me [on Corvo]." Brandão gradually approached and integrated himself into the social universe of Corvo, into its rites and ways of understanding the world. He glimpsed the profound and intimate nature of men and women who were shaped by solitude and silence, by the unstoppable force of time; and he came to conclude that human knowledge on Corvo must be gained through extreme experiences in the complex laboratory of an extreme island: extreme not only because of its dimensions (seventeen square kilometers containing 660 inhabitants) but also because of its distinctive network of interpersonal relations and communitarian social organization, its version of the Portuguese language preserved in one of its historical variants, its isolation ("the vast solitude of the Atlantic"), its stark living conditions. Brandão's chapter on Corvo is dramatic, even tragic. Its constant questioning permits us to reflect on the human condition of these Atlantic islanders: their dramas and intimate complexities, their sufferings and dreams.

As Brandão traveled to other islands in the archipelago, he expanded his vision to include the people of Pico, the figure of the whaler, the shepherd of São Jorge. This last is perhaps the most tragic person in the book, a man without any awareness of his social and personal humiliation. Brandão was able to transform the concrete details of the shepherd's circumstances into a symbol of modern alienation, making him into a monument to all victims of contempt. Contrasting the relative geographical proximity of Corvo and Flores with their social and environmental differences he wrote, "But what a distance separates them!" For in Flores he encountered a society divided into classes: the public servants, the upper class, and the common people. Without an understanding of the competing interests, the small-mindedness inherent in the first two groups, he felt closer to the humbler people, those who waited for the feast of the Espírito Santo to sate their hunger, who wait for the return of King D. Sebastião with the same faith that they await the arrival of the kingdom of heaven.

However, the distance that immediately surprises Brandão is of a different order and it relates to the natural configuration of each island. Brandão, who was a painter as well as a writer, was especially sensitive to variations in the island landscapes: "Corvo dense and bare, Flores, purple and green with purple rocks and its high ground covered in delicate shades of verdant pasture." He lingered to contemplate the colors of the Azores and strove to reproduce the chromatic variety of the landscape, its infinite nuances of shades, as accurately as possible. For instance, the title of his chapter about Flores—"The Sleeping Forest"—conveys the dominance of nature, linking the name of the island to its widespread vegetation, its colors, its silence, its suspension of time, which, in turn, extends to the local social and community life. We feel as if the town were still populated by residents from the nineteenth century. Like the best travel writers, Brandão was able to communicate the singularity of what he had observed. Within a few pages of "The Sleeping Forest" he detailed the varieties of green he encountered: "gentle green," "light green," "voluptuous green," "deep green," "molten greenish-blue," "very green," "dark green," "blackish green." In the words of the scholar Matteo Rei, he "capture[d], like Monet in his multiple versions of Rouen *Cathedral*, the magic and suggestion contained in the space of an instant."[2] To convey his awe before the panorama that he contemplated, Brandão did not describe only the physical exterior but added a subjective dimension that projected his mood. Thus, the landscape of Sete Cidades appears in brief brushstrokes as "a little

---

[2] Matteo Rei, "Fissare l'incanto: Raul Brandão e il diário di un viaggio atlantico," in *La spugna è la mia anima: Omaggio a Piero Ceccucci* (Firenze University Press, 2016), 229.

blue, a little green, a mellow idyll," and the "landscape [of Flores] is serene in character, with a little touch of sadness." Seen from Pico, "Sao Jorge is opaque, dusted with light and dreamlike," just as light and color transform Flores "into an isle of dreams." This immaterialization of the real becomes even more evident in his description of Sete Cidades: "In front of me, an abyss opens up that casts us out of life, to unexpected regions of the dream world."

Speaking to an interviewer two days after his return to Lisbon, Brandão commented, "The others passed through there, but . . . they didn't see the Azores." By others he meant the Portuguese intellectuals, experts, and artists who had taken up the invitation from the *Correio dos Açores* and its director José Bruno Carreiro to visit the Azores but who had spent much less time there, sometimes only two or three hours at each port of call. In his view, such a trip could only be undertaken slowly, with the patience to gaze into the souls of men and women. Because of his commitment to that task, *The Unknown Islands* endures.

Urbano Bettencourt
Translated by Mario Pereira

The Unknown Islands

NOTES AND LANDSCAPES

IN THREE LINES

This book was made from travel notes, almost without any revisions. I merely expanded the occasional scene, making every effort not to detract from the freshness of my first impressions. I had heard from a naval officer that the landscape of the archipelago was worthy of that of Japan. And maybe it is . . . I hope I was able to paint with words some of the most scenic parts of the islands, awakening among my readers a desire to see them with their own eyes! . . .

1926

RB

From Lisbon to Corvo

ABOARD THE *SÃO MIGUEL*

As long as we can still see land, we remain riveted—we cannot do otherwise—to the last stretch of sand, to a violet prick of light that fades and eventually disappears on the crest of a wave. One pinprick and the world has come to an end. Ours is now another world. All of us on board fall silent for a moment. The whitened vault is closed, sealing off the blue circumference where spume skims across the swirling waters that surround us: only a gull persists in accompanying us, circling above the ship. The noise of the propeller and the vast, endless desolation . . .

Life on board steamships has lost all the adventure of voyages under sail in olden times: it is life on board the Hotel Francfort,[3] with doorman and all. All the magic of the old

---

[3] A well-known hotel that existed in downtown Lisbon when Brandão was writing (translator's note).

ships has gone, with their spars creaking in the wind and
the lookout getting ready to shin up the mainmast. What is
striking is the powerful churning that never ceases, the large
waves that are ever grayer and more imposing, which the old
ladies in their high feathered hats, seated from port to starboard, while braving the Atlantic, do their best to ignore. But
then evening comes, and night falls over this salty desolation:
the sea grows heavy and spits its spray at us; an inky blackness hovers in the sky that penetrates the waters and darkens them. The air is leaden, the seas are turbulent, and there
is a grandeur that I cannot get the measure of. It gets still
darker . . . One can no longer make out the endless waves;
all one can hear is the tireless rumble of the engines and the
bilge pumps, like a great broom sweeping the waters. All
this results in something dark and immoderate, something
threatening and full of voices, which the Hotel Francfort, in
all its banality, cannot remove from our minds. The stars in
the shifting atmosphere seem like other stars, the sky another
sky, and I have never felt the unleashed forces of chaos as
closely as today, in this monotonous voice emerging from
the blackness, in this liquid mass that bares its teeth on the
crests of waves amid the inky flatness of this vast, desolate
solitude. This all ends in complete darkness. It is there—it is
present throughout the endless night. Of course, we pretend
not to notice this cataclysmic emptiness, this fateful gloom,
but I feel it next to me all through the night. All through the
night, this complicated thing that is a ship propelled by steam
groans alarmingly as if it were on the point of falling apart;
all through the night, I listen to the water beating against the
hull, and the engines throbbing against my chest. The idea
of death never leaves us: we are separated from the chaos by
a bulkhead with a thickness of goodness knows how many
inches. All the passengers feign absence of concern. Only

over there, under the forecastle (where the third class is situated), wrapped in a shawl and sitting on a tin trunk, that
humble woman feels the terror of the sea as I do—and does
not conceal it. She looks petrified. There is only one thing to
do here, and that is to surrender to it . . .

June 9

But today I awaken, go up on deck, and am overcome with
intense joy. All this, all this blue, all this freshness, invades my
eyes and my soul. The inky blue sea is not only in swell—it
quivers with tiny live grains, extraordinary in their activity,
and the world around me, in permanent renewal, penetrates
me with its breath and infuses me with its vitality.

I take possession of the ship. First, it is the porthole
that delights me, that round, blue eye that gazes at me the
moment I awaken and through which the sea peeps into my
cabin. Then, it is the tiny white cubicle where all the items
have been measured and calculated to fit perfectly, each in
their appropriate place. The cabin has the bare minimum
required and its geometrical beauty consists in its being neither too big nor too small: it has precisely enough room for
a passenger or a monk. When I step out of the cabin, I find
myself immediately on deck. This constricted world can be
crossed in a matter of minutes. But it is in the forecastle,
among the tarred cables, long johns hung up on a line, and
folk traveling in third class, that the most picturesque aspects
of life on board are best revealed. Sailors prepare the winches
for the following day's unloading, the ship's carpenter nails
planks, and the blue waters flow past on either side of the
ship's hull, mingled with surface foam. I look at the first mate
on the bridge directing operations. I return and eventually
spend some minutes contemplating the Ripolin-painted

main deck[4], a coating of white, another of varnish—it smells
of tar and of iodine—until my eyes are drawn to the huge,
uniform mass, only distinguishable from the sky because it
is bluer and more condensed. The view is unchanging, half
sky and half ocean, and down below, on the ship's side, the
bilge water continues to gush out, dispersing into thousands
of liquid pearls; it is the ship's soul welling forth.

To better understand this machine, at once a hotel and an
engine, I have to descend into its interior and contemplate
its inner workings. When we open the iron hatch, the scene
changes immediately. Gone are the hotel and the ship!—what
I see in front of me is a huge space of uncertain dimensions,
illuminated by a light filtered through greasy paper—a huge
temple where whitened skeletons shake. I climb down the
spiral stairs between thick steel columns and cogs that oper-
ate the moving parts like spiders' legs, oil-covered limbs that
move clumsily in all directions. All of these parts which work
in such an ungainly fashion, rising and falling, gleaming with
grease, come and go, move together for a common purpose.
The steps of the stairs are burning, the hot, stifling air throbs,
from time to time interrupted by a deeper blast that stifles
all the other sounds. This complex machinery lights the ship,
transforms the water, and makes the propellers turn. Complex and delicate. "When I'm lying in my bunk," the engineer
tells me, "I know perfectly well which bit of the engine has
gone askew and isn't working properly." But at the very heart
of this means of transport is fire. It is fire that turns the two
great steel shafts that extend through the length of the ship
as far as the propellers. A small iron door is opened and I
step back asphyxiated. Here lies the tragedy of this ship that

---

[4] A commercially produced brand of ready-mixed paint used on ships,
named after the Dutch chemist, Carl Julius Ferdinand Riep, who originally
developed it in the late nineteenth century (translator's note).

has turned into a machine: in order that the hotel may live, digest, and move forward, someone must suffer. I am inside a huge iron pit where the air is unbreathable. There are two smooth gray walls, unblemished from top to bottom. A tenuous, grubby light comes from above, and when those men who live and work down here open the furnace door, they are illuminated by a gush of red light that flashes and then dies away. Cinders burn on the floor, a curved, grimy stoker hurls shovelfuls of coal inside, and the door is slammed shut with a crash against the high iron wall. I steal away. While up above, we live in the Hotel Francfort as if we were in downtown Lisbon, others down below live in the inferno.

June 10

While it is still night, I awaken to the smell of land. I jump out of my berth and go up on deck, which the sailors are sluicing with jets of water. There is a gray, golden light—the blue transparency of the swell, full of tiny sparkles in the distance, and then a more vivid light is born from the great dark mass emerging from the sea under the magic of the rising sun: before me, I see two mighty hillsides, one nearer, its black outline standing out against the golden sky, the other further away, purple and dotted with tiny lights as if someone had blown sparks that had caught and now glittered. The first light reveals the murky stillness of the sea, and as the ship skirts the dark, deformed mass of rock, the flatter lands begin to unfold, and the whole backdrop now appears in its entirety. A puff of blue . . . More trembling light—that first vibrant, fragile light, when the earth awakens and the sea awakens with the sky all pristine and gold in the east, casting its breath into our faces. The freshness that pervades us also renders us transcendent. Over there, everything is still golden and blurred, the hillside all the greater and darker, while next to me all is gray and blue. Reflections and froth drift by in the water, and behind us, from where the ship has come, the sun's light still glitters in the water, mingling with the mist and a wisp of smoke from the funnel that hangs, unmoving, in the air. This is a unique moment, both golden with the sea and the sky gilded and pure, while at the same time becoming pale and gray. For a split second, I wish none of this would change . . . We drop anchor and Madeira opens its arms to us, with the Ponta do Garajau headland at one extreme, and the Ponta da Cruz at the other. I can, I fancy, make out some houses, which for the time being remain impalpable, tumbling down from on high as far as the waterfront. Now the gray tone has disappeared, blue and gold predominate, and before me the huge green amphitheater of the mountains rises up like an altar to the sky. It is a precipitous, green, voluptuous range that offers itself to us, languid and verdant. In the middle, a huge hill begins to stand out; behind it, an enormous mountain, devoid of vegetation. Some of the hills descend as far as the lighthouse and the fort perched on a prominent, jagged rock.

I stay on board all day, contemplating Madeira in awe, steeping myself in the spectacle of light that passes from gray to blue, gains countless tones, and changes at every passing moment until late afternoon, when the sea becomes pellucid and the mountains glassy, with a great cloud perched over them. I see the land lose its colors, fade, and disappear, but in the darkness its ever more intense, fruity aroma intoxicates me. By now, the foreground is purple, melting into a gigantic, uncertain stain behind, and the sea in the west heaves like a bosom, still lit by the setting sun. As the ship draws away, the mountain which has gripped my attention seems ever greater and darker:—it rises, erect, and reaches the sky.

We set sail, and the evening comes, night comes, and night falling over the sea is a poignant spectacle. This ceaseless movement of the waves advancing in endless, tight, rolling surges, one after the other, causes me to face up to everything that I most fear in the world—in the universe, as mystery and chance . . . Gone are the colors, the hues—the gold . . . I am that piece of driftwood carried along by the waves, with no destination, always in the same pitch darkness, powerless in the same perpetual movement . . . It is not only the menace, the majesty of the night, the ocean, its voices; it is something else, far worse, making its presence felt—the tragedy of the universe stripped of its flesh and laid bare before our eyes. With all its complexities and its genius, its potent machines, its ideas, and the architecture it has raised and that reaches as far as the heavens—man, at such moments, feels he is worth no more than a speck of soot against this immense dark presence, this ceaseless agitation. This is worse than implacable, it is worse than menacing:—it does not even acknowledge our existence.

At night, the whole ship groans. From time to time, a bigger wave buffets the hull—crash . . . sh! . . . I feel it up against me as I lie in my berth, with its prolonged lament that fills me with terror. Crash . . . sh! . . .—it is the darkness, the vast unknown ocean, the ocean in its entirety. And the long sigh is drawn out and lost in the night, the wind, the depth.

. . . A transparent morning, hesitant and floating like some delicate creature, shrouded in patches of mist. A pale blue sky, lined on the horizon with light clouds. The sea is uncolored, as if made to be inhaled rather than seen, weightless, calm, and diffuse. In the background, there is a vague smudge, enveloped in mist that gradually disperses into a whitened haze . . . There is a hesitancy in things, a fusion, an awakening, as in the world's beginning, before God's hand had separated water, light, and earth from each other. The tone is very pale—almost devoid of color, ethereal. Santa Maria can be glimpsed between the patches of mist: an elongated hill with a lower part, where Vila do Porto stands out, everything blue emerging from blue. As the *S. Miguel* draws near, I notice that the island is bathed in a golden hue, its slopes streaked with dark shadows from top to bottom. Some of these strips are pronounced and heavy, and there are occasional purple smears that gradually become clearer. I am puzzled and it is only when we are almost within hailing distance of the town, Vila do Porto, that I understand: the island is like a lump of toasted rind made of blackened stone, black sand, as if it had passed through the fires of the Inferno, but the rind is covered in creeping, golden broom, broom in full flower, that one can smell from miles away.

I climb a path among devil's snare and *solteiras,* which is what they call geraniums here, and which grow everywhere. There are hills, fields for pasture, and in the distance a higher peak from which one gets a view of the whole island. The village consists of two or three streets and little dwellings, with a church, the ruins of a convent, and the humble estate of Gonçalo Velho.[5] It is isolated and somber—but its rocks, fields, and hollows are full of birds and their cries: jackdaws, black as crows, fly through the air with tidbits in their beaks, and the aloes fill this darkness etched with gold and scent. There are moments when the sun is hidden and this chunk

---

[5] Gonçalo Velho (1400–60) was the navigator credited with the "discovery" of the islands of Santa Maria and São Miguel and their first administrator (translator's note).

of charred crackling rises all the darker from the sea: all that remains is the smell that pervades the earth and the skies.

It is here that the three-masted schooners come to fetch balls of clay for the island of São Miguel, where they are used to manufacture great pitchers, terracotta mugs, bowls of all shapes and designs. Santa Maria not only furnishes the brick-yards of the Azores with clay, but her people also make jugs, pots, and basins in an inconspicuous little alley in the village. The processes are primitive: a man in a murky workshop pre-pares and kneads the clay, which others will gradually model in the pottery. They work with both hand and foot: the foot operating the large wheel that turns the disc on which the still amorphous lump of clay sits, while the hand shapes it.

What does it matter that this is a wilderness where there are occasional water shortages, making it necessary to bring water in from São Miguel by ship for people to slake their thirst? Here, people live and die. And I must say that two things on this primitive island will remain in my memory: the terracotta pot that keeps the water so deliciously cool, and the soothing scent of its broom. I shall remember it for the rest of my life as the sweet-smelling island . . .

By seven in the evening, we have another island in sight, under a heap of billowing clouds, everything the same color, both clouds and the island. Next to it, a dramatic sunset fills the horizon, gilds the tops of its slopes, bursting through the gaps, to fall in beams over the water. I watch the unfolding of this extraordinary, silent drama, while at the same time the air is ablaze with a coppery hue, and gushes of melting gold flow across the vast gunmetal solitude. On the hori-zon, another island extends like a screen, low, immense, and monochrome. But what interests me is the light that has changed; it is the sky that has changed—the fragile light of the Azores, the Azorean sky laden with humidity and padded with clouds that a painter would convey on his canvas, using tiny, horizontal, lead-gray brushstrokes, fleshing them out and piling them ever more tightly as far as the line of the horizon. And it is this light that stays with me and never lets me go, I who live for crystalline light, and awaken each morning thinking about light . . . It illuminates São Miguel (June 13), filtered through a gray dun sky, with Ponta Delgada extending the length of its harbor, with a great violet hill next to it. It illuminates Terceira in the early morning of June 15, next to a pine wood and a fortress, and it stifles me almost to the end of my journey—a changeless sky, a mildewy mist, a light that is so discreet that things lose their impact and their definition.

The mornings are extraordinary. The tones are neutral—almost always the same lifeless hue—soft, pale mists . . . In this still air, even sound itself is muffled: the world is enveloped in a poultice of raw cotton; a tenuous vapor erases the colors, immobilizes the scenery, and turns the sea into atmosphere. It is an eternal day of the dead, withdrawn and watchful, in which the wind has ceased and no longer blows. White and placid, white and soft, a woeful white, a clarity that is so intimate that my own strength is sapped. Yet at the same time, this light, which emerges from the pile of tiny clouds in the sky, shows us delicate features that we have never noticed before: if the sky is veiled, the sea loses its substance and its matt grayness stretches to the cloudy, imprecise line of the horizon; the whiteness disperses in the water, just as it does in the air, and it only needs a thin thread of blue to filter through the clouds for weary life to smile hesitantly, a feeble smile that suddenly transforms it before immediately stealing away in fear. Certain features of the land are rendered dream-like, others ghostly and ready to evaporate into the air at the first puff of breath.

. . . Little by little, the light makes its presence felt. There are more blanched and gray tones, pale shadows with watery reflections. In the sky, there is the faintest golden backdrop mixed in with the white, benumbed and sad, and almost indiscernible. Things begin to gain shape—but in this delicate light, any change is equally delicate. All movement is stealthy. The whitish gray is streaked with purple, leaving the shadows indistinct; the pure white turns yellow and then immediately regrets its change; the blue begins to prevail a little in the air, and, in the background, the watery greens shimmer, uncertain which color they should assume—blue or purple . . . It is a unique moment, in which new, almost ethereal hues are born into the uniform whiteness, while the sky defends itself, giving full emphasis to its white, with a range of gray tones through which gold attempts to penetrate. At this point, the landscape and even life itself seem fluid and abstract: the wide vista, in grays and white with diffuse, wispy patches, hovers over the infinite grayness of the sea, aglow with embers against its gray . . .

Abstraction and delusion. For, during this endless day-break, we imagine more than we see. We wander. Slowly, the scene turns blue in tone—a faded blue, a blue full of water. We wander enveloped in blue through a world full of white shadows, tepid breath, fluttering feathers. There is some-thing perfect about it, something uncreated and serene . . .

What would I not give for a life like this that can never be fully revealed, and which, for that very reason, possesses an unrivaled allure—full of hushed shades of white and gray! And yet its effects are the least of it—everything lies in the intimacy of this extraordinary light. So faint! So rarefied! So vaporous and soulful! Just abstraction and apprehension . . . It is another world, a world that leaves us perplexed. It is another world, in which feelings are to be suppressed—inhabited by ghosts that smile and then vanish. There are stretches of ocean that are pristine: we do not know whether they are of foam or ash—and pieces of land that are mysterious. A world that is only white and gray, a lifeless world, unable to reveal itself, irresolute—and whose charm is communicated to us through our soul rather than our eyes . . .

The ship drops anchor off Terceira, in a vast semicircular bay, closed on its northern side by Monte Brasil and on its other by the Ilha das Cabras, or Island of Goats. There is a heavy heat. I pause to look at the city, from where a yellow pyramid rises up, the monument to King Pedro IV.[6] Further away, there are one or two bare hills. It is Braga, Braga with greater symmetry in its streets, more whitewash on the walls of its buildings, a Braga that, on a whim, has become a sea-side town, its convents and austere churches extending down to the shoreline, with a fort at either end. In the street, the women wear black capes, fastened around the waist so that they form a shell over the head, while lower-class girls wear a scarf tied with a single knot, leaving their hair visible:—these are single girls; married women hide their hair and tie their scarves with a double knot. It was here that I saw the prettiest women in the Azores—peninsular types, with black hair and sparkling dark eyes.

---

[6] Pedro, as the former Emperor Pedro I of Brazil, led a successful liberal revolt, originating in the Azores in 1832, against the absolutist regime of his brother, Miguel, in Lisbon. He subsequently became Pedro IV (translator's note).

I strike off down a little road, where nasturtiums and pink valerian sprout from the walls. I pass the sparkling white Urze, walk down the narrow lanes through Figueiras Pretas and Bico de Cabo Verde, nestling among pine trees and acacias, which they call jack-of-all-trades here. I continue, among the island's roseleaf brambles. Along the way, I encounter an oxcart—lustrous oxen, the tips of their horns in golden sheaths, and led by strong, stout men.

I enter a friend's garden. I have always enjoyed losing myself in farms and gardens among plots of rustic cultivation. I sit in an orchard full of delicious ripe yellow loquats; the red are sourer, the white sweeter, bursting into juice in the mouth. The vegetation gains a veneer and gleams once more. I glimpse a sheltered corner with stunted vines that produce the light red *cheiro* wine as well as the well-known white from two varieties of grape, the Isabelle and the Verdelho. And then I pass through a silent, humid garden, along alleyways of tall mock-orange trees. In this tepid, diffuse light, I glimpse gigantic pyramids of camellias; the water lily with its yellow or pale milky flower nestled among leaves that stretch over the surface of the green, putrid pond water; the sweet-smelling oleander, which drops its red petals one by one onto a carpet of grass, where they fade slowly as if shedding their blood. This grows before my eyes in an atmosphere that is sultry and in a light that is so verdant that it overcomes the gray. Gardens are always a work of art, and the more chaotic they are, the more beautiful. I have to admit that they enthrall me far more than those monumental gardens where architecture superimposes itself on nature, and that instill respect in me—I feel more at ease in kitchen gardens full of cabbages and flowers. I have just discovered, just here on the right, a kitchen garden. I sit in a row where opaque mallow grows next to parsley. There are pumpkins and flowers, corn and hydrangeas, and a little stone bench

from where one can listen to the trickle of water. It is only
a drop, but it fills me with longing . . . All I need is a young
girl to give me a smile. It just needs the flash of a white dress
to appear fleetingly behind the orange trees. But there isn't
a soul. I must climb further up, to the spot in the Prazeres
estate where one can view both sea and land. In the distance,
one can see São Jorge and Pico and, nearer, the serene dark-
green plots of cultivated land, and, among the little white
houses of São Mateus, the singular church built to provide
solace for those suffering hunger and deprivation. One can
see the Terra Chã, and in the background the bulky Santa
Bárbara Hill. The greenery tumbles down as far as the seashore. I take my leave ever so slowly, so as not to disturb the
noble ferns, a bright red bush called a poinsettia, which gazes
at me full of flowers (and I don't know what to say to it)—
slowly so as not to disturb this leafy silence where we feel as
if we are plunging into soft flesh, warmed by an air redolent
of a greenhouse with its panes of glass steamed up. I feel
myself succumbing to Azorean lassitude, and I am told that
when the flowers are in full bloom, the whole island is so
bathed in their perfume that one cannot sleep. One can hear
a sensuous murmur (it is the spores that are beginning to
open), and the sultry air is like a skin caressing our own skin,
weighing upon our breast like a brick.

I board ship in the same light. I find it unsettling and only later
discover its magic. Ten, eleven in the morning, and always the
same tone, the same gentle clarity: the water is a deep green
next to the cliff face; it shimmers with reflections further out,
and the vast gray bay mingles with the sky, unable to escape
the thick slurry of mist that blurs the entire horizon. But in
this seemingly uniform gray, one sees the humid green of the

great unshakable Monte Brasil, and other greens flicker with
metallic reflections and lifeless colors, mingled with a little
of the blue that manages to seep through the clouds. I take
a closer look . . . These violet mountains, even the Island of
Goats, which is fully violet, and whose violet reflections in
the gray sea attract me, emerge from an almost intangible
liquid that is both air and sky. And these somewhat melancholic colors eventually lead me to change my way of thinking . . . I begin to appreciate more the light of the Azores, the
airy light, the molten hills, the stifling, magnetic air, a roll
of thunder ever hanging in suspense, the islands with their
peaks shrouded in cloud, and the hooded women. Everything is in harmony. It is noon. The blue wants to be blue,
but fails, the earth yearns for light, and light merely offers
itself momentarily and then disappears; the fluid waters, the
imprecise horizon quiver, begin to change before our eyes
and then, fearful . . . Silence. A color unable to assume its
color, that speaks of resignation and nostalgia, and forces me
to lower my tone of voice . . .

June 16

In the cold light of four o'clock in the morning, I am faced
with the unique sight of four islands emerging from the sea
at the same time—Graciosa with its delicate green at one
extremity and its dramatic escarpments at the other; Terceira
in the far distance, almost faded from sight; and, closer to
me, behind the mauve screen of São Jorge, which stretches
lengthwise through the waters, the pointed cone of Pico
soars into the skies, crystalline in its transparency. All this in
a clear but at the same time unreal cold, against a glazed sky
in which the etched lines of Pico stand out, with a tiny cloud
almost perched on its extremity. It is only one particular spot
and it is gone in an instant, for the ship does not stop—and, at

that moment, Pico is fully revealed, soaring into the sky, and the violet stains of the islands have their color shot through by the cloud that begins to disperse—while the nearby Graciosa is revealed in all its verdure. The horizon is wide, the sea panoramic in this early morning light. The limpidity of the air lasts for mere seconds: as the sun begins to rise, it begins to stir, endowed with extraordinary life, a great spongy leaden cloud, gilded on its edges. As the sun appears, the mists begin their restless mission.

It is a moment—no more than a moment of transparency and serenity at first light that touches the sky and then pauses, unsure of itself. This icy, dreamlike glint lasts for a second: then ragged clouds billow up over Terceira, now lost in the far distance . . .

As time passes and the ship advances, the islands change position, cliffs get nearer or further away. I bid farewell to Graciosa—a large plain between two rounded hills, with its whitewashed village in between. Now São Jorge assumes a different position and shape before my awestruck gaze. This long thin island that looks like some great sea creature on the surface of the water, bares its jagged, toothlike rocks at me on its snout. By now, it is bathed in the sun. But I already know that this is not the best light through which to view the archipelago. The sun is worse than shadow. The headlands that stick out into the sea take on a harsh, aggressive, almost blackened air . . . It is ten o'clock: a slim white cloud has cut Pico in half and its cone sticks up out of the cloud, miraculously suspended in midair. One can already distinguish the hills of

Faial, wrapped in mist like raw cotton. We approach the massive bulwark of São Jorge that stands perpendicular over the
sea. Some of the rock faces are fragmented. At the top, there
are lush green pastures. As we get nearer, the intimidating
cliffs seem greater and more formidable, and then, immediately after we have rounded the island's dramatic, forbidding
cape, Pico emerges in its entirety, blue from the turquoise
sea, with Faial on its right, a deep, almost violet blue. And it
is between these pastel stains that we turn sharply round the
cape, which is torn through by slag and riven with imposing,
high plateaus, as if the island had suddenly collapsed. There
are more sheer hills, their sides knocked askew, a black and
red elevation streaked with rust-colored grooves, where volcanic convulsions still throb and one can feel the constant
burbling of the waters—and then the town of Vela heaves
into view at the bottom of a grandiose ravine. The *S. Miguel*
drops anchor, and the darkness of the rocks unfolds into the
darkness of the sea, whose blue tones attempt to flood in but
are blocked: it remains black, reflecting the blackness of the
cliffs. It is a scene from the beginning of the world, a desolate
world of stone and sea. Up there on top, the extensive mist
scatters, sticking only to the rocks, and, when we draw away,
the green of the island's great hills dissipates, while the shadows that travel over the land become distorted, and this piece
of harsh, hostile coastline gradually grows paler, while, on
Pico, one or two clearer streaks become overlaid on the violet
background. I can now make out the hardworking windmills
and the patches of cultivation: in the middle of the island, the
peak, wrapped in its gray mantle, assumes the grandeur of
the mountain where God addressed Moses. A viscous cloud
floats across the earth, lending it majesty, while also distorting it. Next to it, the succession of blue hills on Faial comes
into sharper focus. These great rocks, which change place
and hue, become fused in the surrounding blue, while others

draw nearer and gain volume; this huge spectacle unrolling
before my astonished gaze gives me the impression that the
islands are born from the sea and are being shaped by the
hand of the creator before our very eyes. It is with fervor that
I watch the birth of this huge and ever changing panorama.
I stand at the ship's prow, and reach new islands that emerge
from the waters, born from the mother ocean, dripping with
colors. We pass the two reddish stacks, between Pico and
Faial, which is now a mere stone's throw away. A great green
bluff, hills of a softer green in the background, and a row
of little houses all contemplating me. Another bluff forms
the other limit of the semicircular bay. Add to all this a low,
overcast sky and constant humidity. It is raining. Yet it does
not need to rain: the spongy cloud descends, envelops, and
drenches before dissolving. People and objects must attract
mildew even on the inside.

The night is unreal, a blue night inside the harbor hemmed
in by parapets of darkness with occasional agitated shreds
of color. On one side, that magnetic darkness, whose mystery attracts me—shapes of hills jostling together, but which
fuse into a huge indistinct mass, darker still as the hours go
by. In the background, on the other side of the channel, the
vast triangle of Pico stands out against the pallid light, giving
me the impression of being even more massive and solitary,
like some gigantic figure guarding us from the Atlantic. The
broad highway of moonlight, a scintillating mass of silvery
leaves, flows right up to the ship's hull. From time to time,
there is a shower of rain, falling in a profusion of glittering
jewels. In the distance, a wave begins to gather—its crest
gleaming—and crashes near me in streams of luminescence
that bubble and melt away on every side of the great highway
of moonlight. Another wave takes shape after it, large and
menacing—and now the gleaming crest rises, glistening with
gemstones—to crash in an eddy of light, to melt into light.

Alone on the horizon that great tragic, immobile statue fills the sky with darkness and terror.

While it is still night, we continue our journey to Corvo, with the sea rattling, as they say in the Azores. This channel is angry. At five in the morning of the 17th, we are in sight of two slivers of bluish hue, Flores and Corvo, under a veiled sky and in choppy waters. An hour later, I can clearly make out the truncated bronze cone, with its coppery green streaks high up on its flanks. There is no sign of a tree on that huge lump of rock battered by the waves. It is with some trepidation that I go ashore in the poorest and most isolated place in the world.

Corvo

I want my body to be buried in the cemetery on Corvo, the smallest island in the Azores, and if, for some reason, this is not possible, or even if the executor of my will cannot be bothered to carry out this task, I want my body to be buried in the cemetery of the parish of Margem, which belongs to the district of Gavião; they are good, appreciative folk there, and I like the idea of being surrounded, in my death, by people who, during my life, dared to be appreciative.

(FROM THE LAST WILL AND TESTAMENT
OF MOUZINHO DA SILVEIRA)

June 17

Black stone, black sand, and a greenish sea, which during winter assaults this huge sheer rock with an endless succession of breakers, its craggy cliffs tumbling into the depths, corroded by the waters in a ceaseless, doleful roar. The sky is very low, the clouds white. Ferocity, solitude, and bleakness.

One sole settlement consisting of half a dozen fetid, cobbled village lanes, some no more than half a meter wide, where manure is made. The church, a tiny square, and immediately behind the village, the intimidating mountain, rising up in terraces and slumped to one side. The same flames devoured all of this: the interiors, the walls, the roofs. Elderly women with headscarves, and, over these, a dark shawl, and barefoot men with bonnets and carrying sticks. From time to time, a woman's face, or the snout of a cow, appears at a small window. The gloomy houses, where humans and oxen live side by side, reek of milk and the cowshed. The boys smell of cattle. Around these hovels, half a dozen plots of rye and wheat, divided by dry stone walls. It is all so humble, so abject, so remote, that I am filled with fear. Nothing but a rock and the wind in the vast solitude of the Atlantic.

There is no market, nor inn. There is no doctor, nor dispensary, nor jail. The doors have no key. There are no rich nor poor, and in this isolated world, it makes no difference: the richest man on Corvo walks around barefoot like the others and works the land with his sons. The stonemason is a stonemason and a farmer, the smith is a smith and a farmer, and whoever does not build his cattle pens with his own hands will die of hunger. No one subjects himself to serving others—but all the neighbors help each other out: when the bell tolls to summon them, the people come to replace roof tiles, build a corral, or dig out a terrace.

I look at this place that is so small and so poor, at its patchwork of fields with their dark stone walls, at the tiny threshing floors with millstone and a pole through the middle, to which oxen are attached in order to grind the corn, at the inhabitants and things all of the same, lifeless color; I look at the island stripped of its flesh by the wind, which is so strong in winter that the church bell rings by itself, and I feel as I have never felt before, cut off from the world. What have I come here for? Was it this remote rock in the middle of the ocean with some folk clinging to their plots of land that made me embark on this journey? Was it this residue of a volcano, devoid of scenery or beauty, that brought me here? But there is nothing to see here! Souls as stripped bare as the rock and a life that would be impossible to lead anywhere else except in this world, which is so far removed from everywhere. A natural life? Can man sustain himself by leading a natural life, or does happiness lie in leading a life of artifice? Dressed or naked? Should all our efforts be directed towards illusion and untruth, and is truth stripped down to the bone a sign of inferiority and misfortune? . . . So far away—so alone—so sad! But I take a closer look and remember the words of a man in the throes of debating with his own conscience: "On Corvo, when I sit down at the dinner table, everyone sits down to dinner at the same time, and there is no poor wretch without shelter." In truth, I never saw anyone in rags or in a state of penury. No one has to beg. If someone falls ill, the others tend his land. The poorest are helped out with a piece of cheese to keep them going, and a slaughtered pig is for everyone. The owner of the largest farm harvests a hundred and eighty *alqueires* of corn, and the smallest, forty.

At two o'clock in the morning, in the depths of night, with the roar of the sea ever-present, I hear the cowherd blow his horn to summon the others up through the gate. And off they go together in the dark: they are going to milk the cows at Ribeira Funda, Ribeira da Vaca, and Feijoa dos Negros, uncultivated lands on the northwest of the island, over hills and valleys, where only a few faya and juniper trees grow. Each farmer has two oxen for his oxcart, kept by his front door; the others are out in the corrals, in the open air, until February. The cows, a delightful variety unique to Corvo, are milked in the pastures, and produce that perfumed milk I never tire of drinking and that tastes of all the different grasses that cover the ground like a carpet, and that the cowherds can name one by one: it tastes of berseem clover with its three little thin tipped leaves, of slender hairgrass, ryegrass, hay, bedstraw with its little yellow flowers, *mão-furada, lia vaca, lia vaquinha,* bristlegrass, the white-flowered swine cress, the variety of ferns that they distinguish by name: sawtooth fern, houndstooth fern, pig fern and white-tipped fern—which supply whole layers of grazing in this humidity distilled from the sky. They are milked twice a day—the milk is sucked, as they say—and the whole line of people only begin to descend the steep slope in late afternoon. It is the whole population processing, as I saw in a huge stone altarpiece carved with a chisel by a folk artist—the shepherd boys, the girls carrying gourds on their hip, the women carrying loads on their head, and the old folk, by now exhausted. A hardy, time-honored scene, but at the same time an expression of pain and resignation. And along with the people returning each day from their toil in the fields, I see the tools of their labor—the baskets, the ropes, the picks. And together with the people, the animals, the sheep, the oxen, the loaded donkeys, and the pigs being brought back to their pens, complete the great altarpiece hewn into the stone of Corvo. This desolate rock produces corn, wheat, and wool, with which it sustains and clothes, but most of the arable lands are in the vale of Fojo, on a flat stretch of soil by the sea, two hours away, and the grazing lands are even further away. All the islanders live in the village so as to escape the vast solitude. All of them work on that harsh craggy rock like chiseled bronze, in the little crannies where soil has accumulated—all of them walk barefoot, twice a day, along the rough path leading to the interior. It is a hard life.

"We sow and the wind blows it away!"

The wind is a never-ending worry for these folk.

"It is the most powerful force in the world!"

Above all, it is a hard life for the womenfolk, who climb up to the higher ground every day, a two-league trek, with their pick over their shoulder, returning in the afternoon to make their cheeses and look after the children. They are active, resourceful women. All of them dress the wool and spin it, and almost all of them, by means of a rudimentary loom, make the cloth they and their men wear. And they spin and weave very well. All the clothes on the island are cut by their hands, and of those girls who cannot cut cloth, they say, "Poor wee thing, she's not much use!" It is they who keep the key to the box. The man gives them the money from the oxen, and they take charge of it. And if ever there is a woman whom the man mistrusts, the other women immediately exclaim, bewildered:

"Oh, Jesus, Mary, and Joseph! And to think she's with him!"

The fact is that this business of controlling the key to the box is a very serious matter in these farming communities. The storage box, always made from hard wood so that mice cannot get in, and on Corvo from fossilized cedar, which can be dug up, or from the planks of wrecked ships washed up on the coast, the box is the item of furniture where the best pieces of cloth are kept, the coins that are saved up, the articles of greatest use and value, and the mementos of the dead. The box is passed on as an inheritance. And timeworn by so many hands, it is almost sacred. I have seen country folk die with their eyes fixed on it and the key kept under the mattress. To hold the key is to hold the scepter and prestige. And once it is in the woman's hands, no one will be able to prise it away from her . . .

June 20

I am getting used to leaving my door open. On the first night, I was scared. Now, I sleep right the way through the night on a bristlegrass mattress, with the wide-open window allowing in the gentle breeze that smells of the sea and mingles with the untamed aroma of the hills. I also go up and sit with the shepherds and farmers at the Outeiro square, where the Municipal Hall, the Holy Spirit House, and the empty jailhouse (now housing a cow) are situated, and I listen to them sitting in a circle on the stools discussing matters and reaching decisions relating to the land and cultivation. This is where they assemble before setting off for Fojo, or in the afternoon, when they return. I feel small next to António da Ana, with his short gray beard, Santareno, who has the appearance of an apostle, Joaquim Valadão, Manuel Tomás, the cobbler who walks with a limp, the old whalers, with their beards and striped bonnets on their head, all of them of solemn composure—their faces those of saints or beggars, whose features possess a statuesque quality.

"Will you lend me a cartload of wood?"

"Wouldn't I now?!" (What are you on about now?!)

"So?"

"Two, even."

"Tidy!" (Good, all the better.)

One of them, when I mention the priest, explains:

"He's proper wholesome!"

And the fellow next to me tells me about the death of his little daughter, concluding:

"She died, but wondrous! My wondrous child who's gone to heaven!" (Wondrous is a synonym for happy).

All this is said with pauses and penetrating silences—all these figures in a circle and looking at me, and in a language that is worn like old coins passed from hand to hand, that no longer have any currency but still tinkle with a pure sound. The men are statues that are still unhewn, their speech is rudimentary. But their faces and their words express another life that wishes to speak and cannot, another life that I do not understand . . . They say *wonted* for accustomed, they use *holler* for call, *buck* for jump, *happenstance,* etc. We kiss a child and the mother says to us: "God love you! God pay you!"

They exclaim: "Go whistle before God!"(Go to hell but God
be with you!). And they say things and use terms that I have
never heard before and are completely unknown to me.

The mayor is there, rugged and barefoot like the rest of
them, the district administrator and two dozen old unshod
men, figures from another century, speaking a disentombed
language. I gaze at those huge, gnarled hands leaning on their
sticks, at their burnished timber beards, at the faces chiseled
by a master sculptor who never got around to finishing his
work, and it strikes me that I have already seen all this on
altarpieces or in nativity scenes. They belong to other ages.
By the fixity of their look, they seem fired by feelings and
ideas that are alien to our world. They have been molded over
the years by solitude and silence. I find them almost fearsome,
as if the past had started to observe me, question me. They
all but berate me (or am I berating myself?) for my frivolity.
One of these farmers looks Herculean and another has huge,
craggy, barely human hands, hands fashioned from the soil.

What is alive before me is history, the past. They are the
men of parley and consent, the parliaments that assembled out
in the open, in churchyards, in the country areas of old Portugal, and who may still meet in isolated parts of the north,
such as Barroso, when each village was a tiny republic with
its people's assembly, the *chamada,* which oversaw planting
by fixing its schedule, clearing paths, carrying out repairs on
the mill or the community oven, resolving disputes and prob-
lems of water supply. Nor must we forget that when dividing
up the land for sowing, one part belonged to God and was
dug by everyone.

"Well, now . . . ," one of them says to me.

I awaken to my surroundings.

"Well, now what?!"

And that is all! I look at the sky—the same low, gray sky, the
oxen that trudge sedately past on their way to the millstone

to grind the corn, and I have to focus once again on these men who endure such a harsh, monotonous life, repeating the same gestures every day and the same half-dozen words until they die. I can hear Time lurking out there . . . Here, there is only one thing to do: not to look outside, but rather into people's souls. There has never been a murder or a robbery on Corvo. "No one has ever killed anyone here!" they exclaim with pride. The doors of the mills are always open, for anyone to go and get their flour after it has been ground. "Even today, my front door doesn't have a lock," the largest landowner on the island tells me. "If something is found along the path, it is hung on a nail on the church door. Family is sacred and the girls are chaste. Major issues are resolved on Sundays, in the churchyard, by the priest and the island's elders. When an inhabitant of Corvo dies, four of his fellow residents volunteer to dig his grave and carry the coffin— which is for common use—to the cemetery. The other villagers accompany the dead. I have never witnessed such an extraordinary sense of equality as on this island. Corvo is a Christian democracy made up of farmers."

Words end here, the world I know ends here: here, in the midst of this terrifying isolation where life's artifices are reduced to the minimum, only the eternal survives. One cannot flee the monotony of existence, the solitude that encircles us, the massive architecture of the hills that squeeze and crush us. Ever-present the harsh, restless expanse of the waves and the forlorn loneliness of the village. Months pass without any news of the world, and communication with Flores is by beacons lit on the higher ground, for the channel is wide and so dangerous that dead fish are washed up on the beach in winter. It is here that Time assumes extraordinary

proportions. I see before me its monstrous figure, that which
we eliminate from our futile existence, avoiding and forget-
ting it, but which on Corvo, presides over every single one
of life's actions. Corvo has no influence in the world, but
nowhere else have I felt so deeply the reality and influence of
Time. Everyone goes about their daily life under its domin-
ion, repeating the same gestures and words, and bearing the
same burden, without raising their head or unleashing cries
of protest.

These shorn, tragic figures are as formidable as an insol-
uble riddle. They appear before me and I lay everything else
aside, forget everything, in order to question them. And it
is not that they can answer me—I am the one who needs to
answer myself, for this is what brought me to Corvo.

Is it the wilderness that makes them great? Is it their mea-
ger, harsh life? There is nothing worse than to put a few men
in a boat in the midst of the solitude of the sea. After a time,
they end up hating each other. They have nothing to say and
loathe each other. Imagine what it would be like to cast them
onto this rock and leave them alone on it for ever: after a
while, they would kill each other. Solitude is bitter—man is
a brute. When Rousseau sets off into the forest, he is seeking
and indeed finds a scene from the primeval age of humanity
and, comparing natural man with civilized man, and showing
his assumed perfection to be the true cause of all his unhap-
piness, he exclaims: "Fools, who forever complain about
nature, know that all your failings originate within you!"
Nature in all its starkness terrifies, nature by itself impels us to
horrifying acts of instinct. Contrary to what Rousseau says,
what we must do is to expel nature to the farthest limits and
focus on ideal man. God deliver us from unadulterated man,
left to his own devices in the face of his tragedy, confronted
by chance and the absurd—from the man who is subjugated
by the most basic needs on an outcrop in the middle of the

ocean, left to extract from it all that is necessary for life without being able to raise his head! I now acknowledge in these figures, carved with an adze, another type of expressiveness, and I read in their gaze an angst that they themselves are unable to articulate . . . The black man, surrounded by abundance, never experienced such a curse—it was this man here who was doomed to solitude and toil. The most basic thing in life is not bread, it is something else without which one might as well die. Man's basic need is a dream through which to transform himself.

Perhaps Chateaubriand is right when he makes the following outrageous statement: "What is certain is that no one can enjoy all the faculties of his spirit alone, unless he is free of the material concerns of his existence—which is only possible in those countries where material tasks and activities are carried out by slaves." All civilization is the product of pain. In order to sustain a life of culture, without which we cannot excel, it is necessary for many to suffer. We can no longer conceive of life without art, without fine-quality books, without theater auditoria—this side of Armageddon. But we need to ask those less fortunate for their opinion, consult them and also consult our own consciences so as to find out whether all this material progress has been made at the expense of our moral and spiritual progress . . .

What frees them in their solitude from nature and from hell is religion. It is this that shows them a more exalted quality of life, beyond their dire, monotonous existence. It is religion that unites them and is their salvation.

I understand less and less about human existence! . . . So if religion produces this—this pure man—why are we complicating life? Christ is here—Christ and poverty—Christ even more despoiled than they are—a Christ who fills us with fear. All of them poor, all barefoot, all devoid of any expressiveness. And no one who stands out, not so much as a scream,

no sign of rebellion! This man is a product of isolation and
of religion, and it is the rules of Catholicism that ensure the
dull uniformity of their souls. Subordination, obedience, the
absence of protest . . . In spite of the beauty of sacrifice, there
is something missing here . . . No one stands out from the,
flock. Is the Devil as necessary in this world as God to stop us
from all yawning together from fatigue and for certain indi-
viduals to articulate out loud their rebellion and despair, to
yell at the heavens and torture themselves in the face of the
unfathomable nature of the universe by daring to raise their
head—inspiring such astonishment in their fellow men, that
they cannot look away?!

Or is it that everything is fruitless? Is everything empty
and fruitless?—a cry before this phantasmagorical spectacle
of a vast world. Hemmed in by unseeing forces—and in the
presence of a monstrous god who has had his eyes plucked
out so as not to see? . . . A cry and nothing more . . .

I now know that these men with their faces like those depicted
on altar screens, their huge bones and cracked hands, fill me
with fear . . . Theirs is a particular kind of expression—the
expression of beings who live under the iron yoke of time
and of primitive needs. I also know what is important on
Corvo: it is not the timeworn customs nor the stark life—
what is important is Life itself: the dead and the living are of
one single substance: the dead, the living, and the stone. The
dead, the living, and Christ. We are completely different in
our words, feelings, and ideas. Which of us is better? Whose
is the truly authentic life? Theirs or ours? . . . Elsewhere, I
ignore and cast aside these ideas—just as I ignore and cast
aside time. But here, the idea of God and of death are always
with me, and I watch time's hourglass measure out its sand as

life flows by. The island is poor and bare, the silence is frightening, and the isolation complete, enclosed on all sides by a tormented sea. In truth, I could not live like these men here, but at the hour of my death, I would like to be one of them.

June 22

On Corvo, there are no roads—nor do they want them. I climb the only steep path that leads to the interior, between desolate hills, and divided by dry-stone walls, so many of them that they seem to be the island's natural vegetation. These are the pastures for fattening up the oxen and bullocks. Clutching a metal-tipped staff, I cross the Pastelos, where, on *fleece days* (as they call them), they shear sheep. These are fallow lands, with more hills covered in dark heather, more forbidding hills. A damp cloud lingers over the high ground— the ground is drenched in humidity. It is the unchanging kingdom of grass. After walking for two hours, I reach the crater of Monte Gordo, a perfect, round, circus ring, and with such regular water channels that it is as if it were manmade.

Down below glisten the waters of a lake, with one or two little islands—the archipelago consisting of the islets of Morcego and Mato, and the islands of Manquinho, Braço, Bracinho, and Marreca. There is no sign of a tree, only close-cropped grass and red bulrushes. The low, vaporous sky hovers over the edges of this vast cauldron. The steep slopes are light green, descending deep into the crater, with thin streaks of thick white moss and fossilized strips of slag originating at the very top and ending in the silent water below. On one of the shores, a vague, white, ghostly shape has become a feature of the landscape. I look at this gigantic coliseum. Stones, large pebbles covered in lichen, purple like huge flowers, have been hurled haphazardly all around. The regularity of this vast excavation with its symmetrical rim, the strange tone of its great round clumps of white moss, its soaring cliffs striped with bronze and shades of green right down to the bottom, the serenity of its flat waters, frozen and ghost-like, the crystal-cold light and the unyielding solitude under a sky perched right over our heads, suddenly transport me to another planet, to the interior of a lunar crater, to a dream world, inhabited by white terns that flutter high above us like pieces of down. The pearly mist sinks slowly from the rim, floats along the cliffs, moistening them all, invades and smothers the cauldron, transforming it into a world of chimera, endowing it with personality and life, to once again lift, gradually and in silence, revealing at first the lake, with its little islands floating like calcified monsters, then the whole of the crater's floor, then the huge cliffs in all their grandeur. The guiding trait of this hollowed ruin, this ghostly world of which only a few shards remain, can only be silence. It is the country of eternal silence, a crater nourished by another light, with a rudimentary vegetation of mosses and lichens: the Lake of Dreams must be like this, beyond the icy ether, on the inert white shell of the Moon . . .

One can begin to hear the mournful voice of the wind, groaning, acquiring a frightening resonance down here, as it screams and wails up on the heights, as if it were the voice of the crater itself praying to the heavens. This barren land-scape, these scattered rocks with their pale purplish tone, the mist that tinges everything with blue and billows magically over the clumps of white moss, swooping down to the smooth, flat water, and then upwards to the crater's rim, to hang over it like an awning, affords a view of an unworldly scene, from which I can barely avert my gaze. I find it hard to comprehend; I cannot quite identify with the life of this monstrous, hidden thing in the middle of the ocean, the pre-serve of birds and herdsmen. I feel within me some vague apprehension, some fear of interrupting this great silence and even managing to hear its immense muteness. I lean on the rock and contemplate this mystery, until we set off once more down the steep path to the other part of the island. One or two stunted trees come into view: the majestic juniper is a shrub that they call a cypress here. The wind stunts its growth: it twists and creaks, it is a hundred years old and no more than five feet tall. Then, there are the clumps of heather and moss, which absorbs and conserves the moisture like a sponge. This is the wildest part of the island, Feijã da Era and the Lomba ravine, where one finds wild goats that look like does, with short, honey-colored fur, a black stripe down their back, bulging eyes, and two straight, sharp little horns with which they defend themselves from dogs. I return via the lower terrain, through cultivated fields, cutting along the valleys of Fojo and Poço de Água.

I notice the great intimacy that exists between these men and animals. Communication between humans and animals must only have been as easy as it is here at the beginning of the world. Domestic animals are more intelligent and allow themselves to be led, from which I conclude that stories about the time when animals spoke are not without truth. In the first place, there is no predatory animal on the island: not even the *açor,* or goshawk, after which the archipelago was named, dares to cross the wide channel between Pico and Flores and Corvo. Secondly, I have never come across a hunter: the only firearm on the island is a shotgun without locks. The tiny cows that are native to the island—and, sadly, they are going to die out—are extraordinarily intelligent and good-tempered: they answer when spoken to; the pigs are released in the morning, they leave through the gate, and go up into the hills to earn their living, and, in the evening, they return home. The birds are unafraid of humans. No one harms them. The gray warbler, with its dark crest, sings perched on the end of a branch every evening, right up close

to me. The timid starlings fly around in flocks, feeding on
the husks of wheat, without any fear whatsoever. White sea
eagles stop here. In the channel, alongside turtles, swim thousands of shearwaters, gorging on the shoals of jack mackerel,
before retreating to the rocky outcrops, where they entertain
themselves all night long like gossiping old women, in conversation about the weather, the sea, the fish, in such a way
that we begin to understand them perfectly, so much so that
I shall one day reproduce it if I live long enough. Terns lay
their eggs in the great crater, arriving in April and leaving
again in September. One could say that men and animals are
all united in their extraordinarily mild disposition, subject as
they are to the same rigorous laws of nature. Even those wild
goats become friendly after a few days of close proximity.

We continue our trek and the walls reappear, the time-
less corrals with their narrow corridor, which they call a funnel, and the gate, a hole through which the cattle enter, and
which the herders block with stones, and the pigsty, where
the bullocks are kept at night—and all along the path I follow,
the sea accompanies me on one side, while on the other there
is this impenetrable labyrinth of splintered rocks laid on top
of each other. Girls offer us warm, frothy milk out of gourds,
and shout at the cows, "Mind yourself, blondie!" in order to
get them to stand with their hind legs apart so as to make
milking easier.

June 23

I have never before encountered country folk who communicate with me so directly: there is always a wall of guile or
inertia to break down. With these people, it is not the case.
They look us straight in the eye and speak to us without any
inhibition. No hypocrisy. A lady called Emília tells me: "This
was the priest's house; I was with him so much that he gave

me a baby." And less than fifty years ago, girls took a bath, naked, in front of everyone.

At night, they come and talk to me at the house where I sleep. The light is sparse: in front of me, Hilário, the captain of the port, one or two women, and, hidden in the shadows, faces that, when they come close to the candle, stand out full of contour and character: there is the mouth wishing to speak, the hand that disappears again into the darkness . . . They all have a family air about them. Manuel Tomás, a man of seventy-five, short gray beard, little eyes already misted over by age, one of the largest landholders on the island, tells me about Corvo in days gone by:

"Hunger! Great hunger! . . . The island was going through vexed times: we paid the landlord in Lisbon forty *moios* of wheat and eighty *mil réis* in money. Folk—I can still remember—wore long breeches, with woolen pants over the top, dyed black with madder root and a jacket round their shoulders, a full beard and a cap on their head. There was no lamplight. What light we had came from a flame lit on an ear of flax and, when that went out, we went and fetched a lamp from the church . . . Hunger! Great hunger! All we had to eat were tiger nuts, a plant that gives a little seed in the earth that pigs feed on. We would mill it using a stone and make flour and cakes . . . Sometimes, a piece of land would be exchanged for a tiger-nut cake. Hunger!"[7]

---

[7] "In May, the islanders of Corvo came to Terceira to show the philosopher the black bread they were eating, and to ask for protection against the scourge. It was a scene from antiquity: it was like one of those Grecian republics of olden times, and Mouzinho in fact a Lycurgus, a Solon, but with doctrines that were the opposite of those of the ancients. In the black bread of the islanders of Corvo, enslaved by the rents paid to the island's leaseholder, the minister saw a true crime, and this overriding idea caused him to embark on an immediate course of action. He did not abolish the tax, but merely reduced it by half, adding: 'The times are changing from

There are people standing in the doorway. They listen from the kitchen, and at the back of the living room there are others listening attentively in the shifting shadow.

"Great hunger!" "And mothers would say: 'Let me have this little tiger-nut cake to keep my children going through the day!' exclaims a singular type of woman, her pale skin stretched over her bones, but with a face full of expression and her eyes covered with such a fine membrane that it resembles the filmy coating of an egg. And she continues: "They even ate the roots of ferns . . . And you should know, sir, this world's greatest error comes from a mistake made by Saint Peter. Our Lord told him one day: Peter, go outside and tell the world, the poor should live off the rich. But Peter went outside, got all muddled, and said: Listen all of you who have ears to hear, the rich should live off the poor!"

Then another woman, who is blowing the embers among the stones in the kitchen, eager to speak, suddenly asks:

"Have you got children, sir?"

"No, I haven't."

"Well, then, it would be better if you died so as to leave me a little something." And she laughs.

A woman by her side, reprimands her:

"Be quiet!"

"It doesn't matter. This gentleman is one of ours."

"There was no money," Manuel Tomás continues.

"Nothing was sold, everything was exchanged. Whoever had a house to build would ring the church bell and the house would get put up in an instant. Soap, tobacco, and blue cloth

---

when it was understood that the land had a value before it was irrigated by men's sweat, nor can there be any contrary conclusion once the drill of analysis begins to penetrate the surface of the world.'" Oliveira Martins, *Portugal Contemporâneo.* The bread referred to was made from tiger nuts (author's note).

were brought by the whalers, and the island folk would give
them onions and potatoes in return. The boys would sign up
on the whaling ships, and the women and the elderly would
be left to work the land. The most people had to eat was rye,
and not much of that, and tiger nuts. The oxen weighed sixty
kilos and sheep's wool was held in common and the shearing
was done by everyone. There was always a judge appointed
by the people, whom everyone obeyed and who organized
the tasks for working the land. There was a lot of hunger and
a lot of wind, which destroyed all the crops, as it has done
this year. The pasture was devastated by disease in September. So we had to resort to the wild barley that only grows
among the rocks, in order to feed the cattle."

"Great hunger! Great hunger!" all the others in the darkness agree.

And then that old woman, wizened and agitated, pushes
to the front, and shouts into my face, possibly because she
thinks I am the taxman:

"And then there are the tithes, sir!"

I take in the figures more closely, the weathered Hilário,
the captain, ruddy and talkative, the older men, all with the
same solemn expression, the stark expression of those who
know what life and death are. And they look at me as if I
were from a different planet.

"And then there are the tithes, sir! . . ."

"And then there was also a woman who ran everything
here. Dona Mariana da Conceição Lopes, the daughter of a
priest, she would go to church dressed in a cape and boots on
her feet, when we were all barefoot. Because of this, she was
held in great respect: everyone started to obey her. She would
say: a person shouldn't boast or complain. If you weep, the
poor take pity and say: poor thing. If you boast, they say:
see what she's got, and she doesn't give us anything! . . .
Goddamned poor! She became the queen of Corvo: she

would give advice, arrange dispensations, and ran things as she saw fit."

"She was a teacher to us."

"Teach us something, sir. What we want is for you to teach us how to be rich!"

"But you teach me some songs from here on Corvo."

And once again, that tall, quick-witted woman says:

"Round here, we sing 'The Robber's Flame,' the song 'Long Tall Rita,' and 'Cows in the Plow,' dances from the olden days. Listen to 'Cows in the Plow':

> *Oh, my cows in the plow*
> *When you feed on weed*
> *Milk, half a ramekin*
> *Not even a cannikin.*
>
> *Nice and fat, nice and pretty*
> *The calves follow behind a' sucklin' . . ."*

The ditty and its words are meaningless—but I see before me a little morning mist, the moistened grass gleaming with dew, and, leading the herd, a clear-eyed shepherdess who looks a little like the animals . . . Our evening has come to an end. Every night, at this time, they leave, when the crickets start to challenge us, talking to each other in their rasping chatter that only ceases in the early morning. It is then that I feel even more intensely the heavy weight of this vast solitude among bare hills, among a people lost in the middle of the sea.

Customs have changed very little. Even today, the people of Corvo prefer barter to selling. The island alone produces all these folk need and more. Dinner is brought to the table in a large bowl, soup with bacon and potatoes. They drink the sweet, scented milk, passed around in a gourd. Milk *never stops working,* as they put it: they drink it in the morning, in late afternoon with soup, and, when at work, *up along,* with bread and cheese. There is no wine, and they slaughter an ox twice a year. The kitchen is dark, with the ash box and grate, the hearth and the stove all covered in soot. Over a tray of cinders, there is the grill and the cooking cauldron; from the ceiling, the bacon hangs from its hook, along with the poles across which cornhusks are laid. The wind blows through all the holes in these primitive houses, with their cedar and plaited-rush frames. They grind their grain for bread in the windmills or by using millstones, these latter situated in dark barns where an ox, trampling its dung, its eyes covered, and lashed to a thick beam called a *castalho,* makes the wheel spin on its wooden pivot. There are five millstones on the island, and each of these has fifty or sixty proprietors, who inherit them from their parents and pass them on to their children. The feeling of ownership is taken to its farthest extremes, to the point where they divide up streets with gates, and fields of no more than half a dozen square meters with loose stone walls. There is only one vestige of communal life, which no one remembers ever existed: wool, which was held in common, is still sheared by everyone. And *fleece day* still survives. On the second Monday in April and the last week in September, the whole population assembles to shear the sheep, which they can distinguish by the incisions in their ears: each family has its own sign recorded in the village council's ledgers.

Everyone submits to the deliberations of the elders and the priest. The vicar's influence is considerable, and, in exchange for his services, they provide him with wheat, rye, and potatoes, and, on an agreed day, they take him milk and make him cheese to last the whole year. In church, the womenfolk, scarves around their head, occupy the middle section of the nave, separated by wooden balustrades, and, when mass finishes, they wait for the men to vacate the main altar and the door into the churchyard, before they leave. There is a special aura of respect in church. After a marriage, guests assemble at the bride and groom's home, around the table, upon which there are boiled eggs, wine, and overnight bread. And they start eating, putting the shells to one side, while solemnly commenting to each other: "Manna from Heaven!" They dance until the bell rings for mass on the following morning, with the young couple ever-present and closely guarded by the family—for they hold Our Lord in their hearts—and it is only on the following day that they are allowed to sleep together.

There are no fishermen: whoever wants fish grabs a line and goes and catches it.

"Going for fish?"

"Hey," as if the reply were "yes."

The sea is very bountiful. I have seen them catch wreckfish, with protruding eyes, the size of young boys, sea bream, bonito, barracuda, rockfish, oilfish, black bream, cow sharks, which they take to render their livers to make oil for lamps. I have also seen them catch parrotfish, the males red with a black mark down their spine, the females gray, blue butterfish, which has a lot of bones, grouper, rainbow wrasse, baby skates, snapper, dogfish, scorpionfish, and mackerel. The crew divide the catch up in equal shares, which they call *wages*. And apart from lines, they use cast nets, hurling them into the water and holding the end of the rope round their arm. There are a lot of old folk here who take to the sea like striplings, possibly because they spend much of their lives in the open air and drink a lot of milk. Xexa is ninety-three, Catarina Vicente ninety-one, Ana Canoca ninety-six, her hair still black, Machada is eighty-five, Fraga and Lourenço Jorge are eighty-seven. One of them gives me a toothless laugh and says: "I don't have any teeth, nor do I need them." He drinks milk. If they fall ill, they take to their bed, live on milk, and wait for their health to return, or for death.

The climate is harsh. In winter, niter encrusts itself in the skin of men and in stones. It rains almost all the time. It rains the day after I arrive, it rains on 19th and 20th and, even on sunny days, there is a puff of clouds over the island and a whole wall of it all along the skyline. When we awaken in the morning, the sky is always cloudy; if they clear by ten o'clock, we shall have sun; if not, the day will remain lined with mists. Strong winds sweep over the hillside. The sky changes every day and almost every hour of the day. In the afternoon, that thick vaporous sheet detaches itself from the top of the hills and sweeps low over the rocks. Farther away, the blue sky is almost limpid, but the cloud, the origins of which are unknown, takes on all different shapes, and, without ever changing its color, stops and never releases the hills of Corvo from its embrace. Occasionally, it stops and retreats, invading the gullies and valleys, as if endowed with some strange life of its own. There are always clouds, always wind, and, every year, two months of summer. Sometimes, there is a cyclone. Put this together with the never-ending roar of the sea thundering against the cliffs and our souls. The feeling is one of tragedy. Everything bows before the laws of nature on this volcanic rock, rising out of a tumultuous sea, whose granite columns descend to unknown depths; in this place of eternal exile, the realm of Time, where the landscape is unsmiling and the girls do not sing. Every single day, the same things are done from birth until death. There are no questions asked—they live together like brothers: if

someone needs a plow, he goes and gets it from his neighbor.
The laws of necessity impose themselves on Corvo more
than anywhere else I know. Is it solitude that forces them to
this, is it solitude that teaches them to maintain this order,
this discipline, or is it Christian fellow feeling? If we, on the
outside, cannot suppress Time, we put it out of our minds.
Not so with them. It was here, too, that I appreciated fully
the meaning of the word *bread*. Bread needs to be extracted
from stone, or one dies in the middle of a turbulent ocean.
All this is true—all this moves me—but all this is not enough.
I feel locked away in a prison, and I yearn to escape: the
monotony of life here has a grandeur that I cannot bear. I
can no longer stomach natural existence. Nor could I live as
the inhabitants of Corvo do, tied to the living and the dead,
with Time up above presiding over every necessary and fatal
act of their rudimentary life. Are their lives meaningless?
. . . If they were not Christians, they would tear each other
to pieces. I can never rid myself of this tremendous conun-
drum, which stands before me, stark and cloud-covered like
the very rock itself. A fleeting moment and then death. One
minute without any taste to it and then eternity. I need to
have answers to certain questions . . . Is it better for Time
to exist or not to exist? Is it better to suppress it or watch it
flow past me, hour after hour, like an endless tragedy? What
has greater worth: to live poor and ignored with a clear conscience or to get out of life all the enjoyment it can offer us?
It is only much later that one can answer these questions, for
better or worse, with any degree of satisfaction—but which
one of us would not want to reduce the importance of our
material life, with all its advances, in order to enhance our
moral and spiritual life and possess an inner peace like these
rustic folk? All this is so small but so huge, that I watch, and
debate the question with myself, and fruitlessly attempt to
explain it.

Here, there is no sorrow—there is no hunger here—there is no injustice. And yet at the same time, I cannot bear the idea of staying on Corvo, for there is something monastic about life here, as if it were a convent built in the middle of the ocean. There is welfare perhaps—possibly a more pristine life—less suffering maybe—but I too want to be God, even though I may injure myself and suffer!

And this debate, that will not release me from its clutches, fills me with sadness. The rock is dark, vegetation sparse and utilitarian, life is rigorous but led with a religious faith that I have not experienced anywhere else. These creatures, so isolated in the world, are united in their values. In a winter when even the sea eagles, which live at sea, perish if they do not migrate in time, they find refuge in a Christian feeling of brotherhood that enables them to abide the repetition of the same gestures and the same strenuous acts throughout their lives, as well as the abandonment to which they are consigned. Better still: they love their island. When the girls leave for America, they even bid farewell to the rocks, hugging them as they do. Corvo is a world.

The exact population: 660 inhabitants. There were 900—but emigration has taken many away. If America opened its doors, everyone would escape. Even so, Corvo will probably soon be uninhabited. The birth rate is low. For every fifteen to eighteen born, eighteen to twenty die. There are also quite a few mentally retarded people because of inbreeding.

I have read all the papers available in the local administration—those in the council house were destroyed by fire. In effect, there are no records of any crimes and the administrator repeatedly mentions every week, from 1844 onwards: "There have been no incidents. There have been no crimes." I peruse the visiting magistrate's records from 1836: trivial issues of no importance relating to sharing, in which an agreement is always reached. All claims—with very few exceptions—are resolved on the island. Until only a short time ago, prices were as follows: a dozen eggs cost one *vintém*, a chicken one *tostão*, beef eight hundred *réis* per *arroba*.[8]

The inhabitants of Corvo want nothing from the state except for a new battery for their telegraph transmitter so that they can communicate with the outside world and answer requests for information from passing ships. Note that there already is a telegraph station and an operator, but for years it has not been possible to communicate with them because of the lack of a battery, and because of this ships have been wrecked because they have not been able to answer questions about which coast vessels should skirt during storms. As a rule, the supply ship only calls to load and unload during the four summer months, because access is otherwise difficult. In winter, mail is thrown into the water, which the captain of the port then swims out to fetch. During those four or five months, they request permission to load their cattle—which is transported to Lisbon without a fixed price, and is sold here for the highest possible amount, the agent then sending whatever amount he decides back to the island.

---

[8] *Vintém, tostão* and *réis* are all old units of Portuguese currency. The *arroba* was a unit of weight corresponding to about 15 kilos (translator's note).

The Sleeping Forest

Flores and Corvo rise up before each other, separated by a fifteen-mile channel, Corvo dense and bare, Flores purple and green with purple rocks and its high ground covered in delicate shades of verdant pasture. Along the cliffs, there are scattered hamlets, Monte, Fazenda, Cedros, Ponta Ruiva, among rounded hills and hedges of hydrangeas dividing the fields. Down below, there are three dark pinnacles and, further away, some peaks of a deep, almost blackish blue.

The coast gradually gets nearer and there are promontories and dark crags, while the gentle green of the grass becomes ever gentler, standing out from the dense mass, from where there emerge even darker rocky stacks. A shaft of sunlight penetrates the heavy clouds, illuminates and casts its golden sheen before dispersing into sparkling foreground light, while the rest remains hazy. More somber is the thick mass of hills, the outline of the rocky escarpments; only the light-green waters stir below my feet. We enter the harbor of

Santa Cruz between jagged rocks. Two or three very clean streets, the church, the square, the convent, and immediately behind an emerald hill of perfectly regular features like a tumid breast displaying its nipple brazenly to the skies.

July 1

This morning heralds another misty day. With this murky weather, everything awakens in the morning covered in dew, the trees, the corncobs, the flowering clover, the silvery blades of grass, leaves quivering, unable to stand the weight. I gaze in amazement at the voluptuous green hill, streaked with hedges of blue hydrangeas, and with a great leaden cloud hovering over it; the monstrous purple and green cliff, the light laden with humidity and with whitened patches of fog moving sluggishly along and then dissolving into a fine, filtered mist; in the distance, Corvo disappearing in the humid air and then reappearing when the curtain lifts—the strange features of the land, the ephemeral life of the water, the rain, and whimsical weather. This landscape is serene in character, with a little touch of sadness . . . It is always misty and cool, humid, with that voluptuous hill in the background, but it is a chaste landscape, which conceals and reveals itself, a feminine landscape at the precise moment when it bashfully displays its nudity. The rain is delicate, the damp mists are no more than gilded dew lit and shot through by the sun. And when it falls (which is often), it is sprayed from above, pure and cool onto the stifling heat below. Suddenly the sun appears—suddenly everything we see around us changes, like a stage scene, becoming hazy and diffuse.

The clouds in the Azores have a remarkable life to them, a life that I do not quite understand: today, a cloud over Corvo is reminiscent of a magnetic ring. They billow up on the horizon; others emerge in groups, narrow and tapered

at the ends, which they call little whales, and which indicate
a change in the weather. There are dark ones with amazing
shafts of light behind them; there are ones that travel across
the sky with the loftiness of gods . . . I have the impression
that the light on Flores is the most subtle of all the Azores,
a vaporized light that changes sensitively from one hour to
the next. Perhaps it has to do with the colors that are unique
in their quality here, the powdery purple, the green of the
pastures which is always tender and uniform—it has to do,
perhaps, with the mingled capillaries of the sea, the summer
rain, the sun that spills its gold over all this, and these magical clouds that intercept the light, turning purple like great
colored awnings—to then disperse before our very eyes into
curlicues, wispy threads, or ragged shreds . . . All the colors
fuse and eventually fade into gray, leaving but few residues in
the humid atmosphere. Never before have I witnessed surroundings that are so rich in delights, always so diverse and
ever shifting. Gray is the predominant tone—but a gray that
is tinged with hues, where humid colors float, mainly green
and mauve—gushing, washing over green-smeared hills
with brown and mauve. This is what gives the moistened
land its magic, where even the sun seems moist—moist and
golden, so subtle that it barely pierces the gray . . . And then,
a moment of illumination, the panorama breathes, gasps
slowly like a breast, still glistening from its bath and warmed
by the summer, smiling with a blush for having to undo its
blouse for all to see. At other times, everything disappears
or takes on unworldly proportions, and the water drips like
gold. Water, air, and mist join in matrimony to produce this
impression of chaste grayness or else entirely mauve like a
strangely individual work of art.

Such an environment explains why this island should
be given over almost entirely to pastoral agriculture. They
do not cultivate their fields, but simply grow more grass: it

requires the least effort. The cattle that do not provide milk eat abundantly and are fattened up for the market. In summer, they spend day and night out on the *relvas* (the grassy patches); only in winter are they brought inside and kept in the barns. Almost any farmer, no matter how poor, will have three dairy cows. Grass—grass—all the soft grass that grows, is devoured and flows out through the animals' udders. This pure, clean verdure produces a constant flow of milk, which is transformed into butter every day. It does not flow with the abundance of the water through Fazenda or Ribeira, but, in terms of volume, it is far greater. Meat and milk, these are the result of the stifling heat and the persistent cloud that covers the island, clinging to it, keeping it warm and moist. All the villages on the coast, that look out over the sea, have a dozen fields given over to corn and sweet potato, and grow a few ridges of yams, which are necessary for their food. The rest is pasture. All around them, there is always grass, undulating green hillocks. The hills and valleys give them milk, even the craters of the extinct volcanoes, occasionally sheltering a village in their heart, give them milk. A great white gush flows everywhere towards the dairies, where it is turned into butter, and shipped out into the world. The most tiring aspect of the agriculture on Flores is the twice daily milking of the cows, which drag their monstrous udders over the surface of the ground like some illness. From this green and gold transparency, so magical and airy, with great peaks appearing and disappearing amid the unruly clouds— everything almost vaporous—flows warm, white milk, as if the air, the verdure, the rain, the whitened flashes of light, the volatile atmosphere were all converted into milk, and as if this gray and purple otherworldliness that we see in the fast-moving clouds alone, gilded by the sun and replicating all the images around us, were deliberately created to serve as a wet nurse. Everything points towards this end. One sees the grass grow from one day to the next, watered by the sky, under the veiled light of a greenhouse. This is why that huge, voluptuous hill strikes me as being symbolic. It is a swollen breast: from its nipple tilting upwards to the heavens, there springs an endless stream of milk.

Life here is of no interest to me. One or two slim Flores girls, a dark shawl covering their heads, one or two examples of stout male figures—and nothing more. From one island to the other—Corvo and Flores—there are fifteen miles of sea—but what a distance separates them! . . . Here there are clerks in the local treasury—civil servants—landowners and peasants. I understand Corvo, but I do not understand the parochial interests, mulled over again and again, in a tiny, isolated town hundreds of miles from anywhere. At the windows of houses, behind the glass panes, I see the sad countenances of the old, who have been waiting for someone to pass by ever since they became aware of the world—and no one passes by. It is here that habit has put down roots of iron. Oh! Dear God! I come across people buried fifty years ago here on Flores, alive and clinging obstinately to the same words and the same obsessions as in the past, in a shadowy light that encourages the growth of mildew. Perhaps I am in Purgatory here—Hell is further north . . . Certain people who had disappeared in my youth, and of whose whereabouts I was unaware, have been banished to Flores. Even characters from novels! Even Eça's Dona Felicidade lives here, with her bouts of wind, and other antediluvian ladies with brooches at their neck and bellies larger than any bellies one sees elsewhere nowadays![9] I visited a lady of a certain age who has never left home and does not even know what the island's

---

[9] José Maria de Eça de Queirós (1845–1900) was Portugal's greatest exponent of realism in the novel. The bigoted, superstitious Dona Felicidade is a character in his novel, *O Primo Bazilio* (1878) (translator's note).

landscape looks like. There is only one occupation for whoever does not have work to do: sit on the stone benches of the
Misericórdia and wait for death. And in truth, here there is no
difference between being alive and being dead and buried in
the family tomb.

I climb to the tip of that tumid golden breast, the skin of
which is as smooth as the plushest velvet. From the top one
has a panoramic view of part of the island, tree-filled valleys,
the indented coast, the extensive fields of crops down below,
like a scanty patchwork blanket, a lighter patch of wheat, a
yellow patch of ripened rye. From time to time, a shower of
rain approaches from the sea and all this vastness fades or
grows hazy and more remote. Through the vaporous curtain, I can make out the rounded backs of grassy hillocks,
a white cottage from where springs a deathly deep-green
cypress, dark streaks of pine trees, and, little by little, one
glimpses the whole tranquil vastness, the amphitheater of
Ribeira de Barqueiros, the almost black rocky outcrop of
the cliffs, the violet smudge of Corvo, and, at my feet, the
clear outline of the town. The overall impression is one of
freshness and calm, of mists mixed with gold. This damp,
green landscape is like a dream: it reveals itself, shuts itself
off, smiles, and falls asleep . . . There is an all-encompassing
silence (all sound is muffled by the mist), a wide expanse of
grass dripping with moisture, a serene, opaque light.

Two narrow roads a couple of kilometers long end there,
one at Boqueirão, the other at Ribeira da Cruz, winding past
little white cottages, farmsteads, vegetable gardens, fresh,
gleaming piles of corncobs, rows of faya forming a shelter
from the wind. Pastures and more pastures, and the young
bulls lying in the grass, their stomachs full, unable to eat

more. All the animals are sated. From the sloping banks
sprout clumps of geraniums, mallow plants, or glistening
hydrangeas. Still more pasture . . . It is a paradise for cows:
black, yellow, dappled; with great dignity and awareness of
their own importance, they set off, their horns tipped with
gold, their huge udders almost at one with the ground. Others drown themselves in the soft grass, eating and digesting,
sleeping and eating day and night, contemplating passersby
with disdain. Through a cleft one can glimpse the sea, like a
mirror where the whitish light from the clouds is reflected
and, down below, Ribeira de Barqueiros with a screen of very
green hills. All the shades of green are represented here. Full
of freshness and vigor—the molten greenish-blue of the valley floor, the dark green of the *lakes* of yams, the gentle green
of the pastures, and the blackish green of the beech trees, dull
and mellow in the dew. In the other direction, another road
winds through the Alfavacas, cultivated with corn, sweet potatoes, and tobacco, planted in neat rows, their pointed leaves
half open. Always the same humidity and the same color . . .
And this green insinuates itself little by little and pacifically.
Green invades our capacity to see, as does the distant cry of
the blackbirds our hearing, as they chirp ceaselessly in the
trees that screen the fields of corn. This pretty road comes to
a sudden end at the little bay of São Pedro. I wait for the sun
to set, all gold behind the gray clouds; I wait for the magic
of dusk in this light that is always full of surprises. To the
east, the coast unfolds in shades of gray, purple, and black in
the foreground, with a great leaden cloud dispersing over it
and a fissure of clear sky higher up, opening up into a wide,
pink, dreamlike expanse. Through the ragged cloud, there
is a flash of fire—streaks of gold pierce the opaqueness in
an explosion of flames. Down below, the high cliffs tower
over the sea, with green filaments fusing in the waters. In the
background, blue mingles with the purple and burnt black

of great rocky outcrops. And down below, the green shreds
of sea invade the purple, which dilutes everything into the
same overall tone—the waters, the sky, and the jagged, dramatic rocks. One more moment and the drama reaches its
climax: a dusk in which we watch the colors tumbling into an
abyss, one after the other—the blue, purple, lilac, while the
horizon is ablaze. All this darkness falls before my astonished
gaze, turns violet, drowns in mist, dies in a final death rattle
of mauve and gray. And behind the now pitch-black hills, the
billow of clouds rises and expands ceaselessly.

July 5

As there are no roads to go to Lomba, I travel along the coast
by boat. The hillsides tumble down from on high and stop
abruptly to tower over the sea. They become walls of red clay,
volcanic rocks, dramatic stones gnarled with crannies, steep
cliffs covered in heather and yam plants—a vast panorama
that parades before my eyes as the boat progresses. Sometimes there is a crack in the yellowed crust, and through the
violent fissure in the smooth wall (such as at Fajã do Conde)
one catches a glimpse of a little rustic nook that invites reflection . . . Now there are terraces dug in the intimidating cliff
face, now there are steep hillsides threatening to collapse, now
the huge reddish-blue bulwark rises sheer into the sky (and
minute cows graze high up on the edge of the abyss). When
the boat draws near, I gaze at the compact rock, so high that
it inspires fear, I look into the holes piercing it, caverns and
potholes, into the unknown depths of darkness full of voices
and sounds along the infinite mystery of their galleries. But
once we have turned past the Ponta da Caveira, the island
changes in its appearance. The grasslands of Congro, Fajã
de António Vieira, Ribeira da Silva, and Ribeira da Boa Vista
come into view, and ferns cover the entire cliff face, down

which bluish streams of water cascade, gleaming with froth. More tortured stones appear, the thousand ways in which the water shapes the rocks—a stone arch and, nearer to Lomba, the blackened figure of Senhora Dona, inert upon her white pedestal. I land and climb up a little path cut into the rock in steps. Next to me is the abyss. I keep climbing among boswellia and brambles, treading on the lemon verbena and mint, which release their scent when crushed underfoot. I cross fields around the base of a huge, solitary rock, the Touro, and the Fajã stream, which moves primitive millwheels and flows between stones, wetting the white ferns, used for feeding cattle, and spraying the tooth fern and caterpillar plants, used for the animals' bedding, and eventually reflecting all the jagged verdure of its banks in a series of pools that are as smooth as mirrors. Another brief slope and we are in the village of Lomba, isolated from the world, lost in the sea and lost in the hills. A tiny church, a handful of dark houses, one or two sparse fields . . . Not even an echo from the outside world reaches this place.

The only object of devotion for people in the Azores, or at least the most deeply rooted one, is that of the Holy Spirit, whose main purpose is to feed the poor—it is an ancient, time-honored cult, which has disappeared from mainland Portugal, but which still survives in the Azores, having been taken there by the first settlers. The abbey of Paraclete, founded by Abelard with alms from the people, was the first and last church erected in France to the Holy Spirit. I know of no other in the world. In the islands alone, every parish has a house of the Holy Spirit, with its altar and crown, but no images, distinct and independent from the church. The priest tolerates the cult and attends its festivals—but he is collected

from his house and marched between four thick staffs sym-
bolizing the four apostles, in which the people guard him . . .

In the Azores, they say, as does the missionary, P. Marie
H. Taque, in his recent book on the Brazilian interior,[10] that
it was the devout Queen Isabel who introduced the cult of
the Holy Spirit into Portugal. She had tried to erect a church
to the Divine Paraclete, but the work was on the point of
being abandoned because of lack of resources. And so she
invoked her divine protector in a passionate prayer. Upon
finishing it, she issued an order that armfuls of wild roses
should be brought to her every morning, and every morning
as she prayed, the wildflowers in her lap were turned into
gold coins. The cathedral was soon built, and from its stee-
ples and its towers, she sang of the power of the Spirit of
Light and of Love. This devotion was then spread through
the world by our navigators, and even after it became extinct
in the kingdom, where it left no traces as far as I am aware, it
continued in the Brazilian backlands and the Azores, hidden
away like some sect. In the islands and in Brazil, an emperor
is chosen every year to preside over the festival, which lasts
from Easter to Pentecost of the following year. The crowd
fetches him from his home, and takes him with his crown
and scepter to the church, where the priest receives him and
seats him on the throne next to the sanctuary, in the case of
Brazil anointing him as if he were a bishop. However, this
emperor of emperors has a mission imposed upon him by
the poor: to give everyone food on the days of the festival.
He sometimes bankrupts himself in order to fill the bottom-
less stomachs of the parishioners who have chosen him. The

---

[10] *Chez les Paux Rouges.* Gomes de Amorim, in notes on the interior of Brazil appended to one of his plays, the title of which I do not recall, also mentions this same cult of the Holy Spirit in the Brazilian backlands (author's
note).

women carry trays piled with Holy Spirit *roscas* (sweetbread rings); the house belonging to the cult is transformed into a butcher's. Alongside the carts bedecked with foliage, the revelers dance, dressed in red *balandraus* (cloaks) and wearing tall crowns on their head. The festivity varies in detail from one island to the other, just as it varies throughout the Brazilian interior. What does not vary is its extraordinary popular character. It is not the priest who celebrates the cult, but the coarse, unsophisticated people, who parade the Holy Matter in front of the Holy Spirit. The priest merely collaborates. In the Middle Ages, the church tolerated it, and tolerated the Feast of Fools and the Donkey, whose participants entered the church wearing zucchettos, the mass ending with the priest letting out a series of loud brays, to which the people responded with a chorus of even louder brays. The church only began to replace these farces gradually, and in some dioceses they continued for centuries, through the cult of the Trinity, or the cult of the Divine through the worship of Jesus, Mary, Joseph . . .

But even today, the people who organize the festival are involved throughout, for they comment on it and celebrate it, and in the songs and characters admitted into the area of the high altar, the church in its coarsest, most primitive phase is noticeably present. A moment when the past rises, intact, from the grave, with the multitudes who invaded the place of worship, mixing into the ritual, tragedy, mockery, fear of death, and imbuing it with an incredible, ribald *joie de vivre*.

It is the brotherhoods that celebrate the Holy Spirit on the day itself, but those who make a promise and fulfil it receive the crown in their home, and if the recipient is a person of means, he gives the whole parish a huge feast on any Sunday up until Saint Peter's Day. Today, the emperor is an American who has returned to his native land with money and has arranged for two oxen to be slaughtered and four sacks

of flour to be cooked. There is enough for everyone to eat
to their heart's content! The meat and the soup are already
cooked. While it is still night, the cook for the event has
already emptied the first pieces of meat and the soup from
the cauldron into a tureen, and as dawn approaches (the
alpardo, as they call it) a girl has gone out and offered it to the
first person she encounters on the way. During the evening,
the revelers brought the crown to the house of the emperor
and empress amid waving of flags and beating of drums,
and arranged for the altar to be erected in the living room,
decking it with vases of flowers, silk ribbons, gold tassels, and
stacked rows of lit candles. I take a peep. Ghostly figures slip
along the alleyways of the hamlet. From a steep lane, more
shadows emerge. They are all making for the same house,
where the revelers are singing in the dawn, playing the drum
and tambourine, saying seven Hail Marys, all in front of the
Holy Spirit, dancing in a circle with incredible solemnity and
without ever turning their back on the altar. There is a smell
of the hills. The inhabitants of the village are seated in a
ring, the old shepherds kneeling behind me and the smallest
clutching onto the altar steps . . . The skies are represented
on the ceiling by a piece of pink cloth with a golden paper
dove stitched to its middle. All this reaches its climax with the
offering, beginning in a minor key and concluding in a third
major, in accordance with the customs of the past.

"For the souls of the emperor's dead!"

Sights such as these have a profound effect on me. Things
are only grotesque when they have lost their meaning—but
these merrymakers with their cloaks and crowns on their
head are a direct throwback to the past and leave me with
tears in my eyes. Behind me there are people standing on tiptoe. All are craning their necks to get a view. And I read ado-
ration and wonder in the eyes of that tiny shepherd, dressed
in rags, standing attentively at the door, not daring to enter

out of fear, as if he were at the gateway to heaven. He is listening to the verses so as to repeat them in the future.

Straight after this is the supper, each dish being celebrated with the monotonous chant, and, after all this, there is the ceremony of clearing the tables. In the depths of the kitchen, all I can see are bodiless faces looking at me, like those old panels that depicted human souls. They are sons of the soil, made of the soil, begrimed by the soil. I peer outside: pinpricks of light are gradually getting nearer, advancing down gullies and down the hillsides. These are people who have been dressing up and are coming to the *Chamarrita*.[II] Next to me, seated together on a bench, I notice four stern-faced old men, all with a white beard, all of them barefoot, and two of them wearing large, tin-framed spectacles. After some enquiries, I discover that they are the Sebastianists. I hold out my hand and touch them apprehensively to make sure they are alive. Our conversation is a simple one. In those men's eyes, there is an expression of candor and a faith that fills me with respect. There is something different about them. Something extraordinary that makes them stand out—like plebeian gentlemen. It is not their attitude or their huge spectacles. It is their general air. Their spirit. It is their idealism, as ridiculous and as tragic as that of Don Quixote. I do not dare to argue with them. All of them await King Sebastian just as they await the kingdom of heaven, and one of them declares as they bid me farewell: in the year when there are three winters and one summer, King Sebastian will come. And they walk out together through the door, barefoot, grave, clutching their sticks, and living for their unconventional dream. I stand there, looking at them in amazement . . . At the will of the winds; the same day in July, and all the seasons of the

---

[II] A traditional Azorean dance during the Festival of the Holy Spirit (translator's note).

year—sun, rain, heat, cold, thunder, fog . . . Who knows anything at all in this enigmatic world, in this world of the imagination, where we are all lost, clinging to our explanations
and subterfuges? Who knows? . . . I, too, feel affected and lost
in the midst of characters who do not belong to my age, and
whose customs are as ancient as the world.

Everything in this place is structured, from birth to death.
The family is close-knit, the home tidy, and the woman
heeded in all discussions. There are no servants because no
one wants to serve. At the end of a wedding banquet, a little
rosca is brought to the table on a tray. The bride cuts one
side of it with a knife, the groom cuts it from the other—a
sign of equality—and two young girls each take a slice of
the newlyweds' cake and give it to two poor people. When
someone is about to die, their house fills with people: half
the parish turns up to chat and take snuff together. When the
final tragic moment arrives, one of the old women sitting
round the death bed as *avantesmas,* or death witnesses, jumps
on top of the dying person, his eyes already glazed, and hugs
him, repeating, "Jesus! Jesus! Jesus!" in order to frighten away
the evil spirits and force them away from the bed. And the
moment the words "He's dead!" are uttered, there is a deaf-
ening cry from the spectators. In addition, the moment the
person enters their death agony, no more fires are lit and no
more water drunk, the pots are emptied, so that the depart-
ing soul cannot sip from its surface or bathe in its pores.

July 7

From Lomba, I head for Lajes, and from Lajes to Caldei-
ras—in the interior of the island.

What on the island of Flores passes for woodland is a
series of rolling green hills devoid of human population, all
lined with little clumps of hydrangea and azorina, and of

clubmoss, which produces white ears. The streams plunge down from the plateau, flowing and falling in great leaps, carving their way through the soil until they reach the rock-strewn watercourse, almost always hemmed in by gullies and covered with boswellia or beech—Ribeira Funda, Fazenda, Seca, Grande, between Fajãzinha and Fajã Grande, Ponta Delgada, Cascalho, Ribeira da Cruz, Ribeira da Silva, Pomar, Barqueiros, and still other threads of water that give the island its constant shade of green and its gilded voice. Sources spring up everywhere and there are pools and lakes in all the craters, with the exception of Ribeira Seca. The highest point on the island is the Morro Grande (940 meters), which is next to the crater of Água Grande. From there, one can see the ocean all around the island. It is the sea that forms the skyline. One can follow, as one would on a chart, the contours of the land—the angles of the edges, the undulations in the coast-line, the crevices and the elevations. Here and there, clouds emerge from the depths, creep up the slopes, and evapo-rate into the air. This matchless view is ever-changing in its appearance. Mountains, deep gullies gradually slope down to the sea—in shadow or exposed to the light; hills plunge in cataracts—and with the fog, a dreamlike vista is created—a vista of ever more sublime light. In the distance, the ocean is indistinguishable from the sky, to which it is joined by the whitish blur of mist. Not very far away, the Pico Touro rises up, in the middle of a plain known as the Rochão do Junco, where, in a spot called Fonte Frade, there is a spring of the coolest water I have ever tasted (ten degrees in temperature), which then flows like liquid silver among grasses bent over under its weight. This is the path that leads to Fajã Grande, to the spot known as Portal, a vast semicircle of stone, from where one can see down at the bottom of the abyss, four or five hundred meters below, the roofs of the village, the bay, and the sea. One descends by a zigzag footpath carved in the hillside; and, to the left, keeping to the top of the rocks, one reaches the Terreiros, from where one gets a glimpse of the magnificent sight of Fajãzinha studded into the interior of the crater. This term Fajã or Fajãzinha always signifies a cultivated, fertile area of soil subsidence. Here, it was the collapse of a fearsome escarpment that men transformed into vast fields of corn. Two huge waterfalls emanating from Ribeira Grande plunge down into a gorge below with a great roar, dispersing as they roll down into a mist of liquid droplets. One descends the cobbled lane in a *gorjão,* an oxcart with no wheels. Nearby, and also by the sea, there is the tiny hamlet of Ponte at the foot of a colossal rock, which surrounds and appears to crush it. It is as if these tall cliffs were gradually pressing together, leaving only a thin crack for the blue to seep through and, with it, the ability to breathe. A whole series of vistas, landscapes, wastelands, walls of ruined cities, hills, and jagged peaks that eventually disappear behind the ragged shreds of clouds—or solitary hills, uncultivated land and green pastures . . .

The deepest impression left upon me when I left these lands among the volcanoes, villages with the backdrop of a mountain threatening to engulf them, like a wave of stone about to crush their silence, was my fear of isolation: one feels lost and alone forever, faced by the same limited panorama. A whole life spent next to this without the possibility of escape unless to death! One life, another life, another generation deprived of both adventures and dreams. Rather the jungle and its perils, Africa and its mystery! Upon these isolated little pieces of land, there weighs the leaden burden of an even greater silence and endless abandonment . . . All the villages on the coast and facing out to sea wait for ships, news, and returning emigrants—Santa Cruz, Fazenda d'Além da Ribeira, Cedros, Ponta Ruiva, Ponta Delgada, Fajã Grande, Fajãzinha, Mosteiro, Lajedo, Costa, Lajes, Fazenda das Lajes, Lomba, and Caveira. The craters are situated on the western side of the island, with the exception of those at Lajes and Lomba in the southeast—Seca, Água Branca, Comprida, and Funda. Seca is merely a reservoir for winter rains, Água Branca a permanent lake on the surface of the land, Comprida and Funda cut sheer into the scorched rock. The water forms a pool, like black ink, down below. Funda even looks sinister. It is a picture in two colors, a smudged lithograph, awaiting goodness knows what type of catastrophic event. It is shaped like some living creature, of a robust black hue, full of musings and absorbed in its malevolence. It lures us, and we can never forget it, that look that appears human and comes from the most hidden depths, from some subterranean region similar to that which we carry within us, and from which we can never escape very far . . . All these ancient volcanoes are full of life, of birds and fish; reservoirs of water stare up at the sky with a vague, liquid gaze; some of them have transformed their ferocity into grass and provide milk; others harbor villages, and their fields for cultivation are the most fertile on the island.

I shall never forget the fayas in the northern part of the island in full flower, the Ribeira Funda, which flows amid banana trees and yam plants—the red variety with long leaves, the white with a shorter, darker leaf—the slim, rustling poplars lining the streams in their trajectory, the rustic bridge I cross over the murmuring waters below, and the steep slope covered in boswellia and where wild peach trees grow untrammeled. Lajes is still sleeping; one or two shepherds come in from the surrounding countryside, on foot or riding a little donkey, with their pails full of milk. In front of me, I face the backdrop of a serrated hill. It smells of goldenrod, which produces a yellow flower, fuchsia and juniper plants, which cover the loose stone walls, and which, when they open in the morning give off the scent of their first breath, and I ascend

the slope until I reach the stream at Encharro and a narrow
footpath of scorched black earth. A little further on and I
reach the rim of the Caldeira. I have the impression that the
great green lake at the bottom, amid the sheer, heather-clad
cliffs, is looking at me in the same way as I am looking at it,
with a fixed, immobile stare. Water flows in whitish threads
down cracks in the cliffs, without making the slightest sound.
One hears neither birdsong nor the cry of a shepherd, and
the lake seems enthralled and absorbed in the throes of some
profound contemplation. Not even that waterfall in front of
me, through which the Caldeira Rasa is drained, interrupts
the silence. Down below, there isn't a single ripple and, in the
sky, there is a cloud, whose shadow slowly drifts up the slopes.
Further away lie other hills all furrowed by the winter rains,
the rocks of Cabaço, Tabaivos, Pedras d'Alface, Cruzeiro,
Pico de Sete Rios, solitary, deserted, and carved from top to
bottom by caves. Only the heather, in small cypress-colored
clumps, springs from the earth. Only the dark patches of
heather and rosemary, which produces a tiny black berry,
cover the walls of the crater, down as far as the water, which
is of a lighter green, and is perhaps contemplating us with
a judgmental eye. All this is vast, deserted, and mysterious.
And the silence weighs heavily—only now interrupted by the
young cattle grazing to fatten up, and by the bulls that start
to low—moo, moo—under the mute dome of the sky.

July 13

In order to reach Fazenda de Santa Cruz, one has to pass
through the village of Monte, high up on the slopes of Far-
robo, from where one gets a panoramic view that embraces
the village on the one hand and the rocks of Boqueirão,
immersed in gray clouds, on the other. The path unfolds
along the seashore, along a lofty terrace, and at a bend we

suddenly glimpse the violet blur of the high, rocky cliff, emerging from the violet sea, and shrouded in violet, dusty light. Then the little track twists and turns and a vast green hill appears before us, with the Sé promontory towering up into the sky: behind it, the colossal escarpment of Ponta Ruiva, with two little houses perched over the sea, which is of a deeper violet hue. Never before have I seen this violet light, these gradations of purple that seem so impalpable, nor this extraordinary contrast with the green of the hills and cliff faces, covered in almost black heather, with the violet air and the background violet as far as one can see.

It is a strange novelty—violet and green—this wide purplish panorama where I can distinguish thin emerald streaks of pasture. But it is mainly purple; not only the backgrounds, but there is mud in the foreground, of a purple that is almost transparent and glowing like the dying light of day—of a purple that extends from the highest ridges down to the sea and ends in the huge sunset that is entirely purple. Through the shimmering light, one can pick out the fields of grass of a dewy green, the rocky heights down which there are streaks of deep-green yam plants, until the mist grows thicker and everything becomes blurred. Mixed in with all this, the golden light of the sun, whose airy gilded glow only emerges with difficulty from the gathering gloom, but then bursts magnificently in cascades of fire glittering over the purple waters, while the coast, the hills, the island are transformed into an isle of dreams.

One can already hear the sound of the waters of Ribeira and glimpse the village amid the panorama of hills and bluish cliffs. The water of a brook, almost black in color, gushes down from rock to rock until it reaches the blades of a waterwheel. A partially ruined, romantic footbridge joins various terraces with one or two little dry-stone dwellings. The foamy water surges past the millwheels among squat fig trees. The air smells of lemon beebrush, which they call *luísa* here. I climb and then look: immediately behind the whitish village of Fazenda, in a landscape reminiscent of the mountains of Asturias and Covadonga, huge escarpments tower up, of an imposing deep purple hue that contrasts with the gentleness of the fields and the light green of the pastures illuminated by a cool light. These are the Monte da Vigia, the Pico da Sé wrapped in clouds, and Fransiscão, a perfect rocky cone, which tapers ever more sharply to its extremity. The smokiness of the fog seeps in through a gully, banishes the peaks to a distant backdrop, and turns the solid architecture of the hills a deeper shade of violet. When it momentarily grows thinner and fades, then the wide vista of the cordilleras, the outcrops of strangely formed rocks, the jagged peaks return . . . Only in the foreground, a smaller isolated hill remains unchanged in aspect and color, removed as it is from the foggy region: it remains green and immovable, round and verdant, solitary and placid, while the cone of the Pico da Sé changes tone from one minute to the next, transported to the never-never land of dreams.

All of this area seems deserted. I only encounter one thin, solemn countrywoman, who complains of her poverty and tells me:

"A man works and a woman shelters her children behind her underskirt."

She is leading by the hand a little girl, who hides behind her.

"She's a little milksop," she explains.

I notice the diminutive farming cottage, with a lean-to abutting it, built of sticks, where the cornhusks are kept on large pallets to dry, the clean kitchen, with a cupboard, which they call an *amassaria,* or dough store, the bread basin, and the hearth. Here, they make butter, cheese, and new curd.

The lands are rented out by their owners, who live in the town. Crop agriculture is minimal: the hardest part is watering, or, as they put it, "washing," the plots of yams. The worst is the cattle. Whoever has no land to sustain them works other peoples' land in exchange for pasture. In the winter, they feed their oxen with branches of boswellia and dried corn leaves.

And so this thin, solemn woman has no more to say, and takes her leave of me forever with just a few words:

"That's life! We must show patience."

There is nothing tormented or tragic about this figure. She is an impassive, worn-down woman, whose features have been erased from my memory for good—as worn down as a pebble that has been rolled around so much that it has lost all its sharpened edges. Patience . . . The most terrible characters in Life and in Hell are not those who are tormented—they are those whose every feature one forgets.

Patience, I'll have none of it! I am impatient, and cannot understand the concept of patience in the face of penury, slavery, or pain. No patience for me, even at heaven's gates! . . .

I walk along the road that leads to Ribeira without a care in the world, and then, all of a sudden, there is nothing below my feet as I come to an open crevice plunging to the sea below between sheer cliffs. Halfway down this deep, narrow valley, there is a perfect, free-standing cone and, on either side of it, green escarpments abundant with pines, chestnut, and beech. From this vast, tree-covered wall that blocks the valley, in the distance, three strips of azure water plunge noiselessly from a height of three or four hundred meters. In the other direction, there is the carved shape of the bay, its waters unwrinkled, and the sea reflects the whiteness of the clouds until these mingle with the mist on the horizon. That place, far below, seems suddenly isolated from the world, lost

in the universe . . . It is like a place where no one has set
foot since the navigators discovered it—bluish green, rushing bluish-green torrents, with cascades falling the whole
length of the cliff face amid silence and clouds. It is a pristine
landscape. This water has not yet been put to any mundane
task: it is here to complete the unsullied picture that the hills
appear to contemplate in silence. It is a verdant dream that
threatens to merge into the great gray cloud moving sluggishly along the rocky pinnacles—it is a dream that lives in
some elementary solitude, dream and mists that gradually
descend and submerge it. Occasionally, the sun appears, but
the sunlight is a violent, brazen act, like tearing off a veil or
stripping a virgin. Here, there is only the veiled light that
smells of water and the wild, and that I find almost indistinguishable from the magic fluted sound down below, this
ceaseless music of the birds—coo, pee-o-wee—coo, pee-o-
wee—the like of which I have never heard before. I even con-
fuse it with the voice of the humid green scenery, the chaste,
melancholy scenery, only imbued with life and color by the
birdsong. The birds join and weave each strand of humidity,
the constant fog, the unadulterated spirituality, the solitude,
and the half-slumbered dream. All of these elements make up
the voice of the enchanted forest, the submerged forest lost
in some isolated corner of the island. Now it is about to disappear—it is moving further away and smiles, debilitated, in
ever more delicate tones—and as it dies, it is still singing . . .
The tones are green, smudges of trees—moistened, placid,
somnolent greens. Occasionally, the sun gingerly gilds the
fog; it drains away, fuses with the gray and the green, glistens,
dying before my eyes after brushing the slippery foliage, the
hanging droplets, the gray shred of mist imprisoned by the
trees. Only the pinnacles emerge in the distance. I descend
a goat path, amid chestnut trees reminiscent of a romantic
painting—I penetrate the green dampness as far as the rustic

footbridge across the stream. Solitude—the drip-drip of falling droplets—and, under my feet, the softness of the rotting leaves, suffused with the aroma of death.

There is another tone now—another note, in the original tone, and which consists of the drops dripping from the trees. Reticent and melancholic, almost as green as this dank, static green. I can no longer distinguish sound from color, sound from light: everything melds into the sound of tears slowly falling to the ground, because the leaves cannot take the weight—everything merges into this motionless, green forest inserted into this formidable cavity where there is no living soul to be found. There are moments when the weeping is golden and transparent—the rain shower falls gilded and weightless, it falls in spiders' threads—and then straight away the color fades into the gray and all that remains in front of me is the dripping forest, all its shapes dissolved, as the valley escapes into blueness and humidity and is converted into sound, until all that is left of the chaste landscape enclosed among hills, the hidden, futile landscape, is *saudade*—yearning—and the sound of someone who cannot stop weeping—of someone slowly, slowly weeping, golden and gray. This is not a dramatic pain. There is even something innocent in this sadness. It is that unique moment when children switch from crying to laughing, the laughter already emerging in their still watery eyes as they open, and their cheeks still streaked with the tears one wants to wipe away.

To all this can be added, as my walk progresses, the music of the waters that cascade from on high in long azure threads, and that seem immobile, so distant are they, contributing, along with the simultaneous song of hundreds of blackbirds, to the melody the hidden fauns draw from their magic flutes—coo, pee-o-wee—amid the placid, damp verdure. All of this occurs in an opaque light, in which the sound of the water and the song of the birds shimmer and fuse with the greenness of the landscape, which nevertheless does not disturb our attention, mesmerized by the sound of dripping moisture. For a moment, I do not know whether the water is dripping from the leaves of the trees or from the beaks of the birds, and at the same time I feel the distant music of the great waterfalls penetrating both my ears and my eyes as I get nearer to them. It is sacred, pastoral music, the voice of the sleeping forest, its musical dream, that fills me with ecstasy together with the sound of water, the most beautiful, the most limpid sound I know to forget about time and eternity! . . .

The Blue Island

I can already see Horta at the back of the bay which is enclosed by the sides of two hills, Monte Queimado at one extremity and Monte da Espalamaca at the other. It is a one-horse town, as they say, all white and gray. A couple of convents, one or two solid churches, pleasant old provincial houses with wooden verandas and grilles: occasionally the veranda has a tiny lattice door for the woman to talk to her suitor, while crouching on the floor. "I went to the confessional," as the girls say. Deserted lanes and empty streets, crossed from time to time by a blond meteorite; these are the American girls from the cable station, galloping on horseback, the wind in their hair. Here and there, a country house with its·barn next to it. It is a place whose inhabitants are enlightened and hospitable. Opposite Horta, the formidable bulk of Pico . . . From the top of the Monte das Moças, one obtains a better view of the curved bay and of Monte Queimado, which separates it from another smaller cove—Porto Pim.

What gives these islands their unique character is the
hooded cape. We wander down the deserted streets and,
from time to time, a black, unshapen specter emerges from
a doorway, its head covered by a huge hood. The wearers of
these are almost always old women, but young girls, cozily
wrapped in this item of clothing, which varies little from
island to island, manage to endow this monstrous cape with
charm. They are delicate, fair-haired beings and the contrast
emphasizes their slender figures as they hop along like birds,
condemned to their nightmare, like those strange-looking
creatures that carry a carapace on their backs. I begin to find
this peculiar black bulk interesting and have decided that this
is the only outfit Azorean women should be allowed to wear.
As people leave mass, I enjoy watching the line of penitents
emptying into the streets . . . I also come to realize that, while
it is grotesque, it is also comfortable: they can go to morning mass in it, old women clinging to custom can wear it,
and a girl can go and visit a girlfriend in respectable intimacy,
because she is always fully dressed: all she has to do is throw
it over her shoulders. It envelops the whole body, and by pulling the hood forward over her head, she knows that no one
will recognize her. What a woman wearing a hooded cape
must do is to have a good pair of shoes, because while she
is well covered, protected, and impregnable, she can be recognized by her feet; if she is wearing shoes and stockings,
people will know that the woman under the cape is pretty. A
cape is inherited; it is left in wills, and passed on by mothers
to their daughters. Sometimes one cape is used by the whole
family. A woman who suddenly needs to go out will grab it
and put it on without another thought. "This one belonged
to my grandmother," one girl tells me. "It was made from
English cloth, a magnificent cloth that lasts for ages."

Another feature which exerts considerable fascination
here is Pico—so far away that light seems to pierce through

it, so near that it seems to enter everyone's house. In truth, it is like some magical effect of light, a phantom planted there with the sole purpose of deceiving us. It takes on all shades of color: now it is violet, next it is crimson. At each moment, further transformation. The whole sky is golden and Pico is purple. Evening comes, and the huge moon rises from behind that immense rocky elevation, which reaches the sky. It is majestic and magnetic. Its presence is like that of a huge wave about to break over Faial. This night is the stuff of dreams: the clearly defined cone emerges out of the white clouds that skirt it and appear to hold it up in triumph to the sky. Sometimes, in winter, the snow gleams high up on its peak like jewels, and the clouds that give it extraordinary shapes are different. If I lived here, I would want a house and a bed from where I could see only Pico. It would fill my life.

July 18

From Cabeço Gordo, one obtains a view of the whole island: Flamengos in the interior, and the coastal area of Praia do Almoxarife, Pedro Miguel, Ribeirinha, Salão—the grain-growing parts of the island divided into patches of color— Cedros, Praia do Norte, Capelo, Castelo Branco, Feteira, all amid plantations of rye and wheat, and greenish strips of corn. Land is divided up in abundance, and almost all properties belong to owners who have made good. Money from America has made these men independent. Ownership of land is valued in *alqueires*—about four hundred square meters—each producing on average thirty *alqueires* of cereal.[12] The neat, welcoming little dwelling has a round threshing floor of beaten earth next to it, surrounded by basalt

---

[12] The *alqueire* was a pre-metric measure of capacity introduced in medieval times, corresponding to between thirteen and nineteen liters,

boulders to stop the grain from blowing away; an open space
for the water tank, with the opening through which water is
drawn always freshly painted, and the wattle shed for storing
the cart, plows, and sometimes housing the oxen as well. The
land gives them banana trees, pineapple, oranges, tea, and
successive crops of potatoes; on the slopes, one or two vines;
in the more sheltered areas, wheat and corn. The countryside, which is quiet and very peaceful, and of the gentlest
pastel green, is divided into arable and grazing areas, but the
men of Faial are more farmers than they are cowherds.

I watch these weary folk walking along the roads, the
girls carrying cans of milk, the men returning from work
with their wide-brimmed hats, smocks, and staffs, the young
girls returning from the well, dressed, mainly in Capelo and
Praia do Norte, in woolen skirts that they themselves make,
with purple, green, or red hems, a short jacket, a headscarf,
and a straw hat with a small crown and very wide brim, tied
with a black ribbon. Sometimes, a pitcher is broken and they
exclaim, "Oh for my woes! . . ." They laugh, as happy and
discreet as the landscape is mellow. All of these scenes are
enchanting, with their groves of trees, the well, and the little homestead. It is land that is divided, land cultivated with
love by smallholders who have earned it by the sweat of their
brow and have arranged it to their taste, small and neat. It is
not only the light that has given it this color—it is the rewards
of toil—each one surrounded by his little piece of land, a
patch he can gaze at when he opens his eyes in the morning,
and bid goodnight to upon turning in, when everything is
watered, weeded, and sated. But the light enhances the landscape, the light makes the landscape tender, pale, a little sad

---

depending on the region. It also came to denote a measure of area, with
similar wide variations. Here, both meanings are used (translator's note).

and impassive. The nature of this green, this evergreen verdure that slumbers in its lushness, is docile and serene.

I follow the little road sheltered by fayas and intensely green clumps of boswellia, as far as the parish of Flamengos, next to a little basalt bridge over the Conceição stream. The trickle of water flows down past large knots of hydrangeas. This is a land of washerwomen, whom I meet along the way carrying baskets full of clothes on their heads. Even the poorest dwellings have shutters and an air of intimacy and comfort. On the hills, one or two Dutch windmills are in full sail. The smoke emanating from kitchens smells of incense. This landscape wallows as if in a warm bath. In the fields, the oxen lying in the grass gaze at us, allowing the starlings that perch on their heavy heads to catch their flies. Satisfied and at peace, they lie there undisturbed—getting fat. There are no sparrows here, but the starling performs the sparrow's function with great skill. It perches on roofs and often pops up in the fields where the farmers know it well. Other birds fill the crops with joy right down to the shoreline—the stock dove, the wood pigeon, and the rock dove, this latter smaller, although they are both gray, the canary, the chaffinch, the blackbird, the goldfinch, the robin, and the wagtail, which covered the footprints of Our Lady. The robin, which the locals call a *vinagreira* and is the smallest bird on the island, sings like a nightingale. It differs from the warbler, which has a little black crest, in that the top half of its body is dark. The boys say that when the warbler, which normally lays six eggs, lays seven, the last one to hatch is always a robin.

This place was once more prosperous and full of life. All over Horta and in the parish of Flamengos, there were houses, farmsteads full of oranges, plants, and flowers. The São

Lourenço estate, the Silveira estate, the Dabney estate, later abandoned when England stopped buying fruit in Faial, going to get it from the Cape instead.

I wander into some of these gardens. Firstly into the Pilar garden, situated high on a hill, on a terrace which receives the best light in the world. It is an abandoned garden, with large Dutch beech trees, growing so close together that, by early afternoon, it is already as dark as night underneath them. It is from here that I enjoy watching the changing colors of Pico. I wait. It is almost night. Everything is fading into violet, the perfect semicircle of the bay, the shadow of Pico over there in the background, and, behind the city's ashen hue, the dark green of the outlines of the hills against the golden sky. Along the terrace, the hydrangeas fade at the same time as the surrounding landscape fades. The evening dies, bathed in such a melancholic tincture, that I find it hard not to scream to be left on my own. Colors weaken and lose their tone amid a darkness that is not yet darkness, purple in a continual process of transformation and contraction. The valley of Flamengos slumbers, bathed in mist, and Pico is ever-present, like some huge specter awaiting me. The colors of the earth and the sky penetrate each other in delicate tones that gradually fuse into maroon but that hang on before me for one unique moment, pallid and lifeless, suffocated . . . Afterwards, I visit an abandoned house, an untended garden on Monte Queimado. Lichwort grows in the holes in the walls, a root has pushed the front doorstep up . . . What I find interesting about gardens abandoned to the wild is the attitude taken by trees when left to run riot, the secret but nevertheless fierce drama unrolling between half a dozen tree trunks growing in freedom. Finally, I enter another, very different garden, in Flamengos. It is an old garden with huge avenues of camellias. The trunks, twisted from being pruned, the tiny banks of leaves, form thick, impenetrable hedges. It is a sunless day and the dull heat weighs even more heavily in this entrenched silence among sad, leaden trees. At the end of the main avenue, there is an abandoned gazebo. This may have belonged to a poet or a thinker. The gazebo is crumbling, ivy grows in disheveled fashion along its lofty walls. From the lesser avenues that are always closed and that lead in unlikely directions, there comes a smell of sepulchral dampness. This green, subterranean light, that only enters through the cracks in the thick foliage, darkens everything. The man, whose name I do not know, who designed these paths, the roundabouts, the enclosed arbors full of shadow and flowers, allowed for no other plants in his garden except for camellias. He banished all other blooms from here. There are camellias and shadows everywhere, magnificent camellias, white, red, pink, motionless flowers that grow yellow and are gradually shed from their trees. He built even higher walls so that only shadow might feed on this cold flesh—the flesh of the dead, devoid of expression.

This was the dream of a man with an original mind . . . They try to tell me his name, but I do not want to know his name. It was the dream of a man who spent his life planting camellias, even grafting the scent of his camellias into magnolias. When his work was finished, he died. The house passed into other hands, the camellias grew out of all proportion in the island's damp climate. Left to their own devices, they would engulf the house, the avenues, the sky. The absence of its owner is evident in the garden's unkempt state, the grasses, the moss that has invaded it, the melancholy of solitary things. But I like it all the more as it is . . . I can palpably sense the fragility of our acts, I feel the sadness of our ephemeral life, it seems to me that this entire garden of camellias has been transformed into a cemetery of camellias where the poet's dream is buried. What gives me pleasure is that when I leave the garden, I immediately glimpse Pico, which is

eternal. I always encounter it: on turning a corner, on leaving
the house, on jumping out of bed. Today, it has decided to
die, bathed in violet, but before it dies, it passes through all
the various shades of violet. It fades and eventually shrouds
itself in a cloud so that we should not see it breathe its last. I
suspect that it was put there deliberately and at a calculated
distance, so as to attract us and leave us mesmerized. On
moonlit nights it is a motionless white ghost. We wait for it
to stir. On dark nights, it is a tragic, blackened ghost about to
pontificate in the darkness. I spend days contemplating it. On
the 19th, it is hidden by a cloud—by the cloud—that gradually opens, like the curtain on an altar where a mystery is
celebrated every day. On the afternoon of the 26th it is cut in
half by a gray cloud . . . I should explain that all these islands
have their own special cloud, independent of all the other
clouds in the sky, and with a life of their own within the universe. The wind, for example, may be blowing hard, a wind
wiping away every single shred of air, but the cloud is always
there, assuming various shapes and sizes. Today, it is small
and white. In the afternoon, it changes its appearance at the
same time as Pico changes color. I do not know what position
the cloud has taken, for it is blue on top and gold at its base. I
wait for the bewitching hour when this huge mountain rises
up all crimson from the green sea, against a sky that is growing paler and with the pink cloud clutching one of its flanks.
It is a magnificent spectacle—magnificent but subtle: the life
of the cloud and the color of the mountain. At its base, purple stains—the rich green of pine trees and, at the top, the
crimson bonnet, sharp right up to its peak.

July 24

I follow the road, almost always along the coast, which goes
around the entire island. Traveling by car, I see everything

passing as if in a film:—Feteira, with its white belfry, the tamarisk trees along the side of the road, the plots of corn between the cane plantations, and then the little houses of Castelo Branco . . . I try, but am unable, to fix in my mind a little scene that I scarcely have time to take in: a man with a long white beard, leading a pair of yoked oxen trampling wheat on the threshing floor and, next to him, two girls guffawing with laughter. All that I am left with is the impression of joy in the eyes and on the mouth of the old man—and everything disappears in a flash. Hydrangeas, fig trees, the occasional chestnut—and in the background, advancing towards me a tall hill—Capelo. On this gloomy day, the hydrangeas seem bluer and fresher. It is a road of dreams between endless hedgerows. And the motorcar speeds onwards . . . On one side, a great dark hill, Cabeço Verde, emerges, with a village at its base, on the other, the cliffs of Castelo Branco falling away to the sea. I cross the ash gray of the *mistérios*,[13] always between rows of ever bluer hydrangeas. The man who had the idea of lining the roads with these plants should be honored with a statue on the island. Nowhere else do they flourish as they do here: they like an opaque light, humidity and heat—and if they have these, they are in their element. Their blue is the glazed blue of the Azores on clear days. On the dullest days, they replace the sky's color: they are the blue of this misty land and one of its most strikingly beautiful features. Just imagine the gray that melts away and disperses, turning the sky darker, the air more humid, and underneath it all the blue even bluer, the clusters of flowers an ever more intense and fresher hue. They are everywhere: rows of them lining the roads in hedgerows, marking the divisions in the land, and serving as windbreaks for the farm animals. They

---

[13] The name given to the remains of lava flows in the Azores (translator's note).

fill the land with exuberance and blueness. And on the motorcar goes . . . Where do all these little roads lead, bordered by
neat banks of hydrangeas, and down which no one seems to
go? They are like roads of dreams, open only to enchanted
gardens. The motorcar flies along and I see gilded hills rising
before me on the horizon: it is the newly flowered boswellia that looks like gold. The gray *mistérios* unfold between
abundant hydrangeas, ever more hydrangeas, ever bluer
flooding into my eyes. This lovely Capelo road will remain in
my mind's eye for ever, with the lofty Monte Verde and the
Cabeço do Fogo, all red next to it, the strange landscape of a
Japanese screen, which extends along the whole trajectory as
far as Entre Cabeços. At the foot of Cabeço (Monte) Verde,
I am shown a source that sluggishly produces a thin stream
of water that never grows stronger, nor does it ever weaken.
It is called the Sweethearts' Fountain. Here, girls come to fill
their pitchers, for the pitchers take a long time to fill . . . But
it all flashes past and is gone. The ribbon twists and unrolls
again: Norte Pequeno, the poorest village on the island, half
a dozen straw-thatched hovels, and a huge cliff, the Costado
da Nau, fills the entire skyline. Up there, is the whale lookout
post, and in the background, the slim lighthouse, on an arc
of dramatic red rocks. All the cliffs on the island are strange
and threaten to collapse into the waters. Huge stacks rise up
out of the sea, assaulted by waves with a fearsome roar. The
cliff faces are carved in strips and ripped apart by gruesome,
jagged caves, yellow, gray or black in tone, or otherwise
they slope gently down to the sea in cultivated fields, only
to reappear further ahead in the form of colonnades, arches,
the portals of monstrous temples, corroded dark rocks, or
yellowish blowholes of porous stone. Only terns and white
doves inhabit these tortured heights . . . But the automobile
continues along its route and I am left with the sight of the
velvet landscape under a dull, uniform sky, with that red

mountain in the background, which seems to still spew out fire, and a little stretch of sea, which is a delicate shade of violet. Six o'clock. We pass Praia do Norte, and another village dozing among the blue of the hydrangeas, whose name I do not know. Girls tear flowers from the hedgerows and throw them at us. Then the car stops for only a minute at Ribeira das Cabras, in front of a sheer abyss, four hundred meters tall. Far down below there is a purple and green area of flat terrain, next to the crimson waters, whose colors are in harmony with the blackness of the rock and the violet of the hills. It is a quiescent, spectral scene, down at the bottom of the precipice, spreading out in a deep musty tone as far as Monte Verde, kilometers away, and which causes me to stand rooted to the spot, gripped by the unreality of the situation and the color, and by the delicate light from the setting sun dying from some violet and green sickness, amid arabesques of gold and shreds of leaden gray, mournful, other worldly, feverish. The burnt rock glimmers like slate or absorbs the clarity like pumice stone. The purple plain, stained with darker brush strokes, ends at the seashore and in a backdrop of purple mist, and it all dies away under the incredible gilded dome, streaked with ornate rays.

As daylight begins to fade, I suddenly find myself hurrying through Cedros and Salão, the most prosperous parishes on the island, and then Ribeirinha, and I glimpse another aspect of the ever-blue road as it turns even bluer under Judas trees, with the imposing blue mountains streaked with hedgerows in the distance. They are enormous, they are stunted, and the whole clump is one flower. They are round and squat; they form walls and banks. They burst forth everywhere and can be picked by the armful. Suddenly, I get a glimpse of Praia do Almoxarife, sparkling white next to the sea. But I am so dazed that I can see nothing except for the blue that overwhelms me, all the tones of blue that flood my eyes, the deep blue of the hydrangeas—the blue that fills the land and never ends, and is, perhaps, the real sky of the Azores. At first, all I see is a stain, and in the end I can see nothing but a stain. A stain and vigor. An impression of voluptuousness and vigor: an immovable color, full of life that draws me to it. And then, immediately after the sensation of blueness, the most powerful sensation is that of life enveloping us in silence, waiting for something from us, wanting to communicate with us. How is it possible to extract this never-ending torrent of blue from the dry soil? Under the skin we tread upon, is there some inexhaustible river that comes to the surface through the stems of plants? I am tempted to bore a hole in the earth's crust until I reach the colored liquid that forms the island's nucleus, and that tomorrow will rise up through the volcanoes in a final explosion of magical blue. Great heaps of the purest blue, gushing out of the earth, coming up close to us, awaiting us at every corner, smothering us from every direction . . . I used the word pure, but I think I was mistaken: this delicate flesh exposed along the banks of streams, draped naked across the fields, untended along the paths; this flesh that encircles us and eventually invades the whole island and rises up to the heavens—it is voluptuous, demanding our veneration and our kisses—demanding, perhaps, to be violated . . . At the same time it exhausts me . . . A new feeling gradually insinuates itself into me, leaving me alienated and confused. Am I surprised by blue and gray? Wait, wait . . . See how this moist, vague light infiltrates the blue and dilutes it. Blue and gray become mingled. Sometimes, the hydrangeas reappear and are dripping—either that or it is the gray appearing in the form of such transparent gases that they allow us to glimpse a fixed blue ghost behind them . . . Once again the sad, damp landscape returns and complains, before immediately dissolving mournfully. So what is it I feel? Is it fear or apprehension? . . . It is a weary sadness that stems

more from the exuberance of it all than from the gray that
sheds itself silently over all this fragile blue. It is a feeling that
drips like the dew and at the same time fills me with calm. I
feel there is something lacking that I cannot define—but it is
as remote and as airy as the landscape. It is sadness—but not
to the extent of hurting me: the gray grinds my senses into
an opaque light and transforms it into vague yearning.

Next day, I once again cross the parish of Flamengos along
the municipal road, between humble cottages and yellow
ginger lilies. The road climbs and from the top, I get a better view of the modest, green hollow that includes Far-
robo, Santo Amaro, the wide valley of Praia and Chão Frio,
divided up into strips of corn and rye—a sign of abundance
and a peacefulness that is always of a fresh, vivid green,
under a deep blue sky, the glazed enamel sky of the Azores.
I scarcely notice the wooden huts with thickets, neat paths
of hedges, rustic arches of cabbage rose, where the people
of Horta spend summer days, because I am overwhelmed
by the metallic blue road. There is a wall of hydrangeas in
bloom on either side, a wall that accompanies us and never
lets us go. From time to time, I am suddenly faced with the
sunlit vastness, but my eyes remain riveted to the blue wall
cascading from on high. There is not so much as a blemish:
this soft, splendid, blue blur hugs us all the way to Cabeço
Gordo, which we catch sight of through pinewoods, black
acacia trees, and boswellia, and which rises to a height of
950 meters. A chaffinch sings. Another responds, from deep
within the green flesh of the trees, or the blue flesh of the
hedgerows. I tread the ground where wild strawberries grow,
the aroma of which is intoxicating, in order to contemplate
the valley with its lush, humid earth. A dull green, but a green

that is nevertheless always green, having been soaked by the
shower of rain, divided into such light, atomized drops that
it forms part of the air we breathe—subdued scenes, time-
forgotten or caught by surprise in the morning, when the
landscape awakens. Then I gaze at the extraordinary sight of
Pico bursting up out of magnetic clouds, which seem illuminated by a light forged from within their heart. And I focus
even more on this static blue, under a sky that is blue for a
moment and the blue light. There is no end to this. Kilometer
after kilometer of hydrangeas heavy with flowers, which one
feels like entering until the road comes to an end, until the
world comes to an end . . . I climb up to the shrine of Saint
John. The bush makes the going hard; the slopes are covered
with thick undergrowth, broom, African furze, which produces a purple flower, narrow-leaved clover, and rosemary
full of red berries . . . I have before me, on one side, the crater, with a circumference of two leagues and three hundred
meters deep; on the other, the wide vista—sea and land, hills
and valleys—the sea and Pico, an eerie Pico, suspended in the
sky and resting on an ocean of white clouds. It is only a peak,
but the peak is an enormous, towering mountain, because,
as we climb, Pico also grows bigger. I turn round and at my
feet there is a huge greenish-black hole covered in cedar and
heather right down to the pool of stagnant water and greenish slime, from where there emerges a hill with another minute crater of a brownish hue. It is a beautiful, somber sight.
The smaller crater, as perfect as a miniature, merely lends a
certain tenderness to this isolated place: it is like the other
crater's daughter. It is being reared, prepared for God knows
what fate, deep in that poetic, uncultivated hole. If I tear my
gaze away from the crater, I encounter the infinite vastness,
the majestic altar of Pico, the clouds it catches from the sky,
giving them unforeseen shapes, and the flat sea as far as the
horizon, interrupted by the purple slab of São Jorge and the

pale smudge of Graciosa. The violet of the still waters, the pale green of the land, and the glazed sky over it all . . . I take my leave of this lonely abyss. On the cliff opposite, the somber, doleful shadow grows and advances towards the depths. It is returning home, creeping along the wall, preparing to renew its secret nightly confabulation with the crater! . . .

My return in the early evening light is breathtaking. I see Salão and Pedro Miguel, covered in the blue of hydrangeas; I am elated as I travel along the blue road, with Pico in the background and São Jorge on the left forming a vast bay. It is like a darker Bay of Naples, at this hour lit up by a rich array of effects. Down below, there are hills, always hills—not like the stern mountains of Flores with their peaks made all the sharper by the sun's rays, but round and gentle. Torrents of blue plunge down on all sides. Faial slumbers in blue under a gray sky, and with Pico, bathed in violet, next to it.

At night, I am unable to sleep; I am drenched in blue. I go for a walk along the road under the molten light of the moon. Before me lies the abyss of the sea full of stars. The moon has risen in an atmosphere of extraordinary peacefulness, erasing the glitter of the diamonds, but, amid their final reflections, the threadlike sinews of the waves vibrate as they crash against the coastline and then disappear into the gaping hole of night. The moonlight grows stronger and the silence seems to await some supernatural message from us. I look. All the hydrangeas have turned white, a perfect white; all the hydrangeas stare at me, tranquil and white, motionless and white. I step forward apprehensively. It is a landscape without blemish. The blackbirds are deceived on nights like this when the moon is full and blanched, and start to sing in bewilderment. Pico, startled, vast in the moonlight, has swollen and

takes up the entire skyline. I listen . . . I would love to surprise
these flowers that live in this humid, white silence, and discover their mystery. I close my eyes. The obscure existence
of the plants that do not take their eyes off me makes me
lose awareness of my very personality; I sense the existence
of another entranced life, scattered through the world, more
lucid—maybe even more lucid . . . I walk and walk, ever
forward, between whitened ranks, dazzled by the sight of
whiteness and chimera. An American lady was so transfixed,
there wasn't a hand she didn't throw herself at in order to
kiss . . . As for me, I do not have the courage.

I am now frightened of them, so pure and white, as they
offer themselves up to this magnificent white moonlight, a
mute white in which one can feel a subtle, gilded reflection
of the sun. Everything is still; only the bewildered blackbird
sings amid the virginal whiteness. It does not stop until it is
exhausted. And when its beak releases its harmonious ditty,
another unseen blackbird immediately hears it and replies,
continuing to weave this musical arabesque over the rhap-
sodic, white landscape.

Pico

What from a distance was purple and diaphanous, violet and maroon, depending on the light and the weather now, as the boat approaches it, looks dark and disjointed, charred and black, devoured by all the fires of Hell. It is a piece of scorched rind. Never before had such a powerful conflagration melted the stone until it fell in drops and disintegrated into coal dust. It is a picture in black and gray that fills me with fear. Here, there are holes and caverns where the lava formed bluish colonnades and stalactites, great hanging clusters, melted by the heat and solidified by the process of cooling. This island—the largest of the Azores—is blackened to its core, in its very soil, in the pumice stone on its beaches, the dust on its roads, its houses, its fields divided and subdivided by walls of basalt, in its little village churches, sad and seared. The overall impression is one of intense mourning, of great desolation. Volcanic ash fell over this vast piece of land and only occasionally is the blackness interrupted by expanses of flat gray terrain, the so-called *mistérios*, like a patch of leprosy following the fire.

However, the blue is all the bluer in those places where a basalt corridor has an exit route into the vastness of the sea (such as at Furna). The spout which enters it there has an abundance of life. Emerging suddenly from this inferno a chestnut grove, a little plot of corn. Round, squat fig trees, or, from behind a charred wall, there bursts a climbing lilac. Then, there is more rock, more blackness and rock. More desolation and blackness, yet more harsh volcanic rock, which produces tea, coffee, and tropical crops; fruits from the mainland, and oranges and loquats, all the more delicious for their suffering. The dragon tree is huge with an ample canopy, the ferns and bamboos are gigantic. Olive and chestnut trees are cultivated next to wild pineapple, which ripens in the open air and fills the surrounding garden with its perfume. The vines are well known in the outside world. The white wine of Pico, produced from the Verdelho grape and cultivated in the lava, is a drink that has a sour tang to it, and, with its amber color, it looks like fire. Dig out a chunk of lava, fill the remaining hole with some soil, and the vine will put down roots wherever it can, sheltered by the enclosing walls and growing out along the ground over the rounded stones. They only prop up the branches when the grapes are nearly ripe. In its day, Pico produced thousands of barrels of wine, which it used to export almost entirely to Russia.

The two roads that lead out of Madalena along the coast and encircle the island, one ending soon after São Miguel Arcanjo, the other at Lajes, serve some of the parishes on Pico, almost all of which are on the coast, and each one with its own specialty: Santa Luzia is the parish for fig trees, São Roque for wine, Prainha is where corn and wheat are grown, Santo Amaro specializes in boat building, and also produces mats, and Cais do Pico and Lajes are the two great whaling parishes. The men of Pico are the most hardened sailors in the archipelago, weather-beaten, gaunt, stern, and loyal.

Each day, in a kind of crow's nest at the top of a mast up on the high ground, a man watches the sea, eyeglass in hand, waiting for a whale to appear.

One can travel perfectly well along the roads in a two-wheeled buggy, pulled along by a mule, especially in the morning, when the inevitable dew is falling from the leaden sky, and the plants, living as they do in the dry, dark soil, wait all night long, ready to suck it up voluptuously. The air on Pico is a miracle of freshness and subtlety. It rains, and then dries out immediately. This porous stone absorbs the humidity like a sponge.

As the road slopes upwards, the driver jumps to the ground and talks to the mule. The sea is a mirror and the sky is as much a mirror as the sea, with white cotton-like strokes and sluggish clouds, fringed with gray. Everything is so still and white that it is as if time has stopped. I gaze at the sea, with its snail trails and white patches lit up from within. In the distance, the other island, São Jorge, stretched out in its entire length, is visible and ever present. I have come to realize that the most beautiful thing each island has to offer, and that which completes it, is the island opposite—Corvo and Flores, Faial and Pico, Pico and São Jorge, São Jorge and Terceira and Graciosa . . .

As I travel along the road, I am ever more taken with a field of dressed and weeded corn, its straight, green stalks, and with the frequent little patches of garden and the contented hue of their vegetables, the trickle of sparkling water in conversation with the cabbages, as if it were aware of the benefits it is imparting to them: the water seems pious and intelligent, and the vines and the chestnut groves represent the triumph of man over the violent forces of nature in this vast desert with its ravaged rocks. There are places that appear concealed and apprehensive in the midst of such blackness: over there, the green is even greener and the mallow ever brighter next to the wall of burnt stone. I saw two or three villages vibrant with vegetation next to huge, leaden-gray hills, and of these especially São Miguel Arcanjo, which exudes a sensuous air after one's eyes have been invaded by so much blackness. I sat in an overgrown garden with fresh, glossy camellias the size of trees, on a high terrace overlooking the sea and the world. I sat there, oblivious to the hours going by, swathed in blue light, absorbed by the sea full of golden reflections, São Jorge reclining in the sun, distant and bathed in gold, pockmarked with inoffensive, purple craters, their mouths open before me, with a little touch of blue inside them. I progressed along the road, which curves through clumps of trees and hydrangeas of an even more metallic blue than the others, growing in the soot of a fumarole; I sat in the shade of some wide, low chestnut trees and went as far as the dramatic *Baía dos Mistérios,* silent and gray, abandoned and leprous, and further still to Prainha, which I caught sight of from high up on the road, with its vines and tiny wine cellars, on the bay of Canas. Even when this landscape attempts to be joyful, the idea of death and destruction is always prevalent. There is an air of foreboding here that one only feels in Naples, within a picture that is more voluptuous and perfect, with Vesuvius smoking in the background. These hills oppress me. I feel crushed by this dark solitude. I seek out the ocean for relief: the entire coast, with its jagged cliffs as black as pitch, terrifies me. Eventually, I return to the overgrown garden with its moss-covered steps and its splendid terrace. It is a place that invites quiet contemplation . . . There are some houses clinging to the steep lane beside it, and in one of them lives an old whaler, now retired, his white goatee combed into a fan on his gaunt, shaven face. He is the only human presence on this day, an encounter with a mariner ending his existence with his eyes fixed on a past more alive than ever before his eyes. He bought this house among the rocks. He erected a mast in his garden with a weathervane on top to signal to the ships, and he is going to end his days with his turbid gaze gripped by the infinite restlessness to which his entire life was connected. And, in truth, there is nothing more beautiful in the world apart from one thing—the sky; but that is far more distant whereas the sea keeps us close company.

At six in the evening, I return to Cais do Pico, while this piece of charred rind sinks into more sadness and shadow. I cannot take my eyes off São Jorge, illuminated by the last of the sun's rays, streaked with shadows and almost transparent. I sit on the steps of the old Franciscan convent, with the unreal island in front of me. Pico has disappeared, São Jorge is opaque, dusted with light and dreamlike, and I can make out one or two clear craters—one of which has collapsed and is completely blue inside—and hills overlooking the sea, until everything fades into gray and plunges into darkness. I am left with a feeling of melancholy at seeing night fall in some uncongenial village. I feel that the night is hostile towards me. With the fading light, all the shadows have converged on this deserted convent, infiltrating through its open doors. They are rummaging around back there in the cloister. And I almost cry out with cold and alienation . . .

Night time at Cais do Pico, a row of dark houses along the shore, whale carcasses bobbing in the waters, a place you can smell from miles away, bathed in smoke and blubber, adding to my bitter sadness. Someone comes to my succor when he starts telling me about the extraordinary festival of Saint Mark celebrated on April 25 on Pico, Faial, Corvo, and Flores . . . I had already visited the apothecary's shop to examine the jars, one by one, I had already contemplated the humdrum houses and the humdrum inhabitants, I had gone down to the shed full of chunks of blubber, where the whale is rendered down—and my only thought, which became more fixed as the night wore on, was to get away, to get far away from these little provincial hellholes, worse than prison or exile, where folk feel the weight of daily mundane reality, the monotonous routines of daily life, the words that are used every day—, when suddenly everything changed before my astonished eyes, as if convex mirrors were distorting these colorless people, turning them into figures of shock and pain, mockery and pain. Everything is subdued, everything is subject to the same rule, everything subordinated to the same laws—and then on Saint Mark's Day all the rigid gestures are jettisoned, all the carefully chosen words, and another world emerges into the open, more grotesque than carnival, more profound than carnival, because on this day all action is represented by the dead—it is a picture in which one sees the exhausted faces of the revelers and, behind these, other bonelike faces that persistently come to the surface; this is a strange celebration in which, beyond the man, there is another man performing, where the shouting and mockery of the participants belong more to the world of ghosts than to the living. The brotherhood of Saint Mark consists solely of married men, and has erected an altar, with a crown of horns, all lavishly decorated, and with a larger horn sticking out on top. At the door of the association's headquarters, the members lie in wait for the first passerby to come down the gloomy street, grab him, and force him to kiss the crooked emblem.

"Come and kiss the horn, for you deserve it!"

"Our friend here is now in the brotherhood!"

And the others laugh, everyone laughs, and if anyone pro-
tests or struggles, the mockery increases, the laughter gets
more raucous.

All of those bellies shaking seem to be getting bigger, all
of those mouths seem wider. I can see in the eyes of that fat
devil a clarity that does not come from the wine . . . Careful!
. . . This ribaldry is perhaps sacred, firstly because it is secular,
and then because it represents the ugly undertow of humanity, all the repressed mischief that has burst out into laughter,
the misfortune that makes people laugh, the farce that ends
in pain.

Wait for night to fall . . . At night, everyone pours out into
the street clamoring, bearing flares and torches, and not only
do their dark and ruddy faces gain a more dramatic relief, but
this mass of people shrouded in smoke takes on even greater
proportions and seems much larger: all of the ghosts have
answered the call. The president of the association carries
the horn aloft, resting on a mantle supported on four sticks,
clutched by a number of other drunken revelers who have
lost all notion of reality . . . One of them goes ahead, swaying
a thurible in which a shaving from the horn is being burnt,
given him by another ruffian from an incense container . . .
Now the scene is complete: the dense, violent throng stag-
gers drunkenly along—because one of the richest devotees
of Pico has opened up his wine cellar for the use of the brotherhood on this day—the mixture of blackness, smoke, and
red flames, the nocturnal revelry, the surge of the dead and
the living stampeding along narrow streets until they come
across some loner, who, amid all the laughter, is obliged to
kiss that large emblem borne along by the procession.

"This fellow's one of ours!"

"Give it another kiss!"

And the screaming and shouting reaches its height when they arrive in front of the houses they have picked out for special attention—the crowd crosses the whole town on that night. Here, they stop. They call for the brother shut away inside and whom they believe should belong to the association. "Come on! Come on!" At that point, an angry woman appears, opens the door, and showers them with insults:

"Hooligans! My man! . . . I've never given him cause for offence—you're the ones who're doing that! . . ."

The shrieking, the shouts, the guffawing, and the delirium redouble in intensity. The brandished torches wave around in the night; they fill the patches of shadow with smoke and fire, which then assume a shape, and shimmy and dance with the people, becoming part of the festival. The wine-sated paunches sway with pleasure.

"Come on out!"

"Hooray! Hooray!"

"Go home to your wives! Hang your heads in shame!"

"I have already seen this—even better in Rubens's feasts, where naked men and women roar with laughter—in the Flemish paintings of the "Sabbath," in which the devil in the form of a goat presides over nocturnal scenes of delirium and old witches fly through the air riding on broomsticks. It was there that I also saw an extraordinary man laughing with pain—a man I never forgot, a dead man laughing at the living. Is it the strange pleasure of wallowing in the slime that causes these beasts, forced to obey rules and laws during the year, to indulge in the excesses of Saint Mark's Day, or is it the first Flemish settlers on these islands peering through the eyes of the living, and impelling them to carry out acts of profanity? . . .

A pause. The rabble calms down. The sermon begins. The preacher climbs up onto a wall. A rock. A table pulled into the street, and the crowd around him waits for the hidden dissolutes of the parish to be named and shamed. And he does not hold back . . . He is a man of fine words, who first demonstrates the advantages of being part of this honorable association, although some people do not wish to confess to it . . . No one escapes him. But so-and-so—he asks—so well respected, what is he? . . .

"He's a cuckold!" the throng yells enthusiastically.

"So-and-so, our friend and neighbor, where is he supposed to be, I can't see him?"

"Here! . . ."

Hooray! Hip-hip hooray! And the sermon continues until the rabble, with its mantle, its tripod, and its chorus of drunken revelers, slips off down one of the darker lanes and the first light of day dissolves the picture, leaving no traces whatsoever, as if the whole thing belonged to the realm of dreams and nightmares.

And it is this that I find most extraordinary. It ends without leaving any vestiges and it lasts only a few hours. A duty has been fulfilled—it vanishes like a shadow. For a few hours, any notion of reality has been forsaken through the magic arts. The insults traded would have ended in death on any other day. On this day, however, madness and pain walk openly, hand in hand, down the street.

In the morning, everything is in its right place, each one has returned to his usual routine, and voices are no longer raised. This incredibly rowdy party, this noisy frolicking that takes place, violent and unhinged, on the evening of Saint Mark's Day, has disappeared in a puff of air. All that is left is Cais do Pico's row of dark houses, the bloody sea where whale carcasses float, and the stench of blubber that never goes away . . . In the olden days, it was the custom in secretive provincial communities for someone to go up into the hills and broadcast through a loud hailer the scandals of the terrified town—so-and-so is sleeping with such-and-such a woman!—and the echo amplified the sound in the valley floors. Maybe this act was a way of correcting habits and forcing women to take care. But here, it is something different. It is not an individual act; it is the whole population that takes part in this extraordinary feast, clearly focused as if they were carrying out a ritual.[14] Put this scene in the back alleys of Flanders and the maddened mob amid torches and darkness, and in the midst of the mob, that man laughing—the man unable to repress the laugh of malevolence that originates in the sedimented gloom of the human soul—the laugh I try to stifle, but also hear within both him and myself, as if some strange kinship bound me to him, me to evil, despite all the

---

[14] Colonel Afonso Chaves published a most interesting pamphlet on this festival, celebrated in the islands where Flemish settlement was predominant, comparing it to analogous festivals in Flanders:

"Nowadays there are not many localities where this festival is celebrated, and it is evident that its liveliness as a spectacle depends largely on the leaders of the brotherhood.

"On Pico, some years ago, there was a 'devotee' who placed all the wines in his cellar (and they were plentiful) at the disposal of the Brothers of Saint Mark, on 25th April, and that is why the festival on that island achieved considerable renown, just as others may yet achieve, either there or elsewhere, for the same reason.

"On Horta, up until 1870, the nuns of the convent of Glória sent the collegiate members of the parish church out on Saint Mark's Day, before the main litanies were said, carrying a tray with a crown on it made out of tiny sugar-paste horns, with artificial flowers in the middle and a larger horn destined for the vicar.

"During the litany, of which the celebrant was the newest member, and for the purposes of the act was dressed in a red rain cape and led by two singers, these, upon uttering the invocation to Saint Mark, would turn round to the celebrant and bow, to which he would respond with another.

"On the tray with the offering of the nuns of Glória, there were always some verses alluding to the festival for betrayed husbands. The membership thanked them for the gift in writing, and also sent verses referring to the festival." Francisco Afonso Chaves, *As Festas de S. Marcos em Algumas Ilhas dos Açores e a sua Origem Provável* (author's note).

efforts to overcome selfishness and animalistic brutality. Jeers and boos, and that figure I shall never forget. I have done all I can to kill it, but to no avail.

As for Pico, I have lost it. That marvel of black and gray emerging from the very depths of the sea, I have never seen it again, ever since I stepped back onto the mainland. Everything has been reduced to fragments, limited scenes, and little snippets of landscape. I anxiously try to conjure up that initial general impression, but am unable. Have I lost it for good? One does not conjure it up on the ascent made, at two in the morning, from the torrid town of Madalena up to the summit of Pico, with the sky pure and cloudless, as the nights in the Azores almost always are. Pitch-blackness and stars. Two figures accompany the pack animals, Master Narciso and the man carrying supplies. Half asleep, the caravan immerses itself into the icy early-morning air, into the immense open space that envelops it, while the cobbled path is only clipped by the hooves of our mounts. Is that clarity or opaqueness rising up before us as we reach the pasturelands, the vast stretch of terrain that reaches as far as Cabeço Vermelho? After four hours' march, we reach Pedra Mole—an emptiness covered in brush, heather, purple gorse, and a little bluish-white flower—and beyond it an indecisive sea of milky mist which the growing clarity infuses with movement, fluidity, and life. One moment it seems to become denser and then, as the light grows stronger, it takes on the eerie aspect of a white sea, white clouds, a sea of fluff which, from time to time, opens out to reveal a harsh peak, an isolated floating rock. Beyond this vaporous ocean, one can just make out another one that is entirely mauve. Nearer, motionless white clouds, white as ice, stretching like ice floes northward, from the cracks of which trickle threads of blue water. In this

great cotton-bathed solitude, a white mountain rises up in
the distance, while further down more vapors float upwards,
and the sun lights up the tops of the dark hills. For a few
moments, the denser fog that has come from below and rises
with the sun, ever thicker, forms a strange, united sea all the
way to the horizon, a polar white world that leaves us completely isolated. Immobile and cold. I wait, and suddenly I
hear . . . Can you hear it? . . . From the depths of the white
abyss, the tolling of a bell reaches us in the midst of our solitude from below this sea, summoning us to mass.

Perhaps it comes from the Candelária church, in the parish
of São Mateus. In any of the little villages submerged under
the uniform blanket of white cloud. Another bell . . . farther
away, so crystalline and pure that it surprises and enraptures
me. It is a sound that gives an uncommon impression of
life, as if the enchanted bells of Atlantis were beginning to
summon us. Can you hear it? Can you hear?—And almost
immediately, the vaporous curtain opens to reveal the whole
landscape on this violet morning . . .

We sleep in a hollow in order to see the sunrise tomorrow
on the top of Pico. Whoever wants to, sleeps by the light of
the stars. We're off . . . What I seek, for the last time in my
life, is not the vista—rather it is the delight at being free, out
in the open. We light a fire, over which illuminated shadowy
figures bend, there is a smell of heather in the disordered
camp. Everything acquires a new savor, our eyes seek out
the desert rocks as they do when one is twenty, the keen ear
takes in the slightest nocturnal sound, our sight rediscovers
the alertness of primitive life. More, and even better, our soul
finds vital fulfilment in this wild existence for which we were
created, and aspires to the heights. Once again, there is light
before the final plunge into darkness! We are off! . . . The
harsh climb takes another four hours on foot, turning right
and treading a hard stone path, until we reach the base of the

crater, covered in purple vetch and wormseed. The surface vegetation gets smaller: it consists of very low broom, as if it had been clipped. Inside the crater, which is about thirty meters deep, rises lesser Pico, a cone of burnt red stone. It is only possible to climb it on the east-southeast side. The small crater and cracks emit thin wisps of smoke. There are occasional rock falls down the huge cliff on the northern side. It is cold up here in the middle of summer. I wait for full daylight to glimpse the sea and Pico, Faial, São Jorge, Graciosa, and Terceira in the background, almost out of sight. And, more than all this, the vast blue shadow cast by this huge mountain carved out of the sea over there towards the parish of São Mateus. It is an extraordinary ghostlike presence from sunrise through to an hour after the sun has appeared.

Along the southern road to Lajes, the view is darker and harsher, with rolling hillocks the color of slate and the land divided and patched by endless walls of basalt. We pass cindered threshing floors where the bundles of wheat look all the more golden, dwarf chestnuts bursting from the coal-covered earth like basil. And from all this blackness, all this accumulated grime, the occasional bright scarlet flower of a creeper stands out, or a field of fully ripened white corn. A boy on a lookout pole scares away the most daring birds with his sling. It happens all in one movement, the skinny boy, standing erect in classical pose, and the stone leaving the sling with the speed of a bullet in the direction of the flock, which takes to the air, while he, motionless, his arm outstretched, unleashes a raucous cry. The islanders greet us, their straw hats worn over headscarves, leather sandals on their feet, and the bronze-skinned girls drawing water from the wells. The little dwellings are very neat and tidy inside. In some of these gloomy villages, people live just as they did three hundred years ago, with half a dozen ideas and a priest, with the same sentiments as in the past and a priest. The landscape gradually changes. The hills grow in stature and, once again, I glimpse the doleful, desolate Pico.

I pass through Monte, where customs are as untainted as on Corvo, Candelária, and São Mateus, which reminds me of a mining village. The mountains get ever loftier and above a certain height, shorn of all vegetation, consisting only of structure and drama. They are torn, punctured from top to bottom with caves, sculpted by torrents of water. There is harshness and gloom, followed occasionally by the great gray flatness of the *mistérios*. After the *mistério* at the bay, that of São João comes into view, and then the huge *mistério* of Silveira accompanies us for kilometers the length of the road, lending the landscape a fantastic air. This is the true expression of Pico. Gray and black, always gray and black, the blackness of the earth, the blackness of the hills as they grow higher and higher, and the eerie grayness of the *mistérios*, vast necropolises, where earth and stone are buried under the same gray sheet.

It is the mineral landscape that gives this magnetic island its character. The patches of tender green, all the greener and gentler among the scorched volcanic black, have disappeared, and all that is left is this huge area of desolation. I remember that bay—called the *Baía do Mistério*, gray, isolated, and lifeless, every day awaiting the dead, the remains of wrecked sailors dispersed throughout the ocean. All that lingers in my memory are the vast, cadaverous expanses, devoured by leprosy and with a backdrop of skeletal hills.

The *mistério* is the result of eruptions at the base of Pico (the *mistério* of São Jorge, for example) covered by a lichen, *urzela*, or orchil, which grows in vast gray expanses, giving the impression of a leprous scab corroding the earth, of a dead, shrouded world. This is followed by ever taller hills forming an inaccessible barrier alongside it, with leaden gray streaks down their sides, from top to bottom. This vision grips and oppresses me. I am accompanied by this vast cliff that no light is able to tear away from the growing blackness. There is not a single plant! Only hills, ever more massive and forbidding. The light is different, grayer, and the huge backdrop the color of burnt slate seems to be waiting motionlessly for this planet to complete its process of putrefaction.

I am absorbed by this extraordinary mineral landscape, by this vista that has emerged intact from the fiery depths. There is no sign of life—just dead, scorched, useless expanses, whose visual beauty consists largely of the outlines, the solid architecture of the hills whose stern profiles soar into the sky, of the solitude and colors with which they are covered, of the effort displayed by those who scorn all needless detail to brazenly reveal their suffering to God. Here, all of the rocks have been through fire, and so express their charred, static protest. The product of some monstrous birth process, the island was devoured to such an extent that it was on the point of melting away. This is its pain. The pain of the world exhibited to us, paralyzed before our eyes—naked, solitary, mute, tragic pain, without a mask, without so much as a rag to cover it, without a scream. Just pain.

The blackened stone cliffs are followed by sepulchral stone cliffs, with ruddy lacerations, where fire still seems to be at work, the slag still melting, the mineral with its bluish, sinister tones is followed by crags that look beyond hope, their holes ripped apart to reveal their most intimate state. There was no mercy, no moment of respite from that huge, silent torture: everything, from the dust to the mountain, passed through the same inferno and is still releasing smoke in its death throes.

I cannot take my eyes off this vast, dramatic vista, this nightmarish panorama that gives me some inexplicable pleasure. Everything plunges in cascades of black dust, or fused together in one gush down the smooth blue walls, dark with even darker curlicues that look like some undecipherable hieroglyphics—petrified in richer tones, a black the color of blood, fusing into one another until they reach the gray floor. An abyss—a disorderly jumble—a field of debris. And all this on top of the gray chaos.

We cannot escape this. It even imposes itself on our field of vision and these bare bones stripped of all flesh fascinate us, not because of the monstrous, tortured impression they create, but because of an intellectual beauty, the grave, superior beauty that belongs to the realm of the soul.

It is possible that the Azorean light reaches perfection at this point. There is nothing to distract it—only the same tone on this vast picture painted in the same color, only varied by the most delicate nuances of shade from here to infinity. Over the gray of the *mistério* hovers the concentrated gray of the sky—the gray of the clouds washes over the scattered stones. In the distance, the immense rock face emphasizes the severity of this magnificent vista. All of the stones that the chain of iron hills spewed from the earth were covered in ash, which enshrouded this spectral world. It is an abstract landscape, a dead landscape. It is not only the color of the sky, which is the same throughout the islands—it is the color of the stone—, it is a vague feeling of terror—it is the corpse that has remained intact and begun to sprout mold. There is no deformation. On the contrary. There is a new kind of beauty to be found—but once it has been found, it never releases its grip on us . . .

Over there, in the far distance, surfaces of a much darker gray and fields covered only in stones, and musty-colored flowers—everything unmoving, quiet, at a standstill. One neither hears the chirping of a bird nor sees the glint of a trickle of water. The world has died, submerged in grayness. Even the strange light is fading. And ever present is that sinister mountain nearby, which vomited all this profusion of lava, and which seems to be boiling away under the layer of gray. One walks from one side of the road to the other in vain: the *mistério* pursues us silently. Sometimes the stones look like waves, a choppy sea that has turned to gray stone with foam on its surface. The orchil spreads inexorably, covering everything, hills, stones, iron deposits, roadside embankments, turning everything the same uniform color. It is one of the most beautiful sights I have seen—this vision of a planet where living creatures and things have been consumed by dust, leaving their silent, gray phantom to float for evermore in the ether. This vision stays with us and haunts us until we reach Lajes, lost at the base of such a massive hill that it inspires fear. No one can ever avert my eyes from this extraordinary two-tone vision of Pico in gray and black, presiding as it does over the middle of the ocean, and the whole archipelago of the Azores.

A huddle of small dark dwellings, a vast solitude, and a great sadness. The coast forms a bay, closed on one side by a huge, ungainly rock. Lajes is known for whaling—a fleet of six ships and two hundred people employed in whaling. It is surrounded by mountains, which thrust it in the direction of the sea. The lookout's house is high up, in an abandoned mill, in a place known as Terra da Forca (Gallows Hill) . . . Everything here smells of whale and is drenched in whale, everything that is eaten tastes of whale, which is rendered down in huge cauldrons to extract the oil. I ask:

"But aren't you aware of it? This horrible smell?"

"It always smells good to us. It's a sign of money."

I fail to even notice the tiny chapel, which they say was the first to be built on the island. I stand amazed in the middle of the village before an unfinished Gothic cathedral, raising its black basalt ossature into the air. A priest was responsible for such a disproportionate structure in this isolated, hill-bound wilderness—all dreams are disproportionate. He raised its thick, high walls on solid foundations. Every day, he could be seen high up, his cassock flapping in the wind, helping the stone masons as if he were a mason himself—heave—heave—heave ho—pushing the chunks of lava into place. He asked everyone for money, the whalers, the Americans, the rich, the poor, in order to complete his open-vaulted colossus, where the entire village would fit modestly into one tiny corner. He spent his own and other people's money, he worked liked a slave. During his entire life, he had no other idea, ambition, or interest. And when it had reached those dizzy heights, all ready for completion, he dropped dead—and the cathedral remained forever after where it was, abandoned and empty, without a roof, a dark, dead carcass looking out over the sea, and separated from the land by bulky hills threatening to submerge it. Sea birds live there . . . This was a dream, and no dream is ever fulfilled—the world is not big enough for dreams.

Now, I can complete my picture: with its stark, black hills, this incredible backdrop, this lacerated, static, gray panorama, the product of a strange imagination, the grotesque procession of ghosts clamoring from door to door, mouths gaping with laughter; all this has made my stay there over a day and a night worthwhile. This black, deformed island has taken charge of my senses. Everything that at first repelled me, the murkiness, the fire devouring it, the *mistério,* everything seduces me. Pico is the most beautiful, the most extraordinary island in the Azores, of a beauty that is unique, of a marvelous color and possessing an uncanny power of attraction. It is more than an island—it is a statue raised to the sky and shaped by fire—it is another Adamastor,[15] like that of the Cape of all the Storms.

I erase all the different hues in the picture: all I desire before me is Pico, dark and dramatic, eaten away by its ashes that will eventually devour living creatures and things, leaving it alone and proud against the sky, like the carcass of that abandoned cathedral overlooking the beach.

---

[15] Adamastor, the giant of Greek mythology turned to stone by Doris for falling in love with her daughter Tethys, was used to personify the Cape of Good Hope by Camões, in his epic poem, *Os Lusíadas* (1572) (translator's note).

Whaling

High up on his post, the lookout suddenly stood upright, gave the signal of whale ahoy with his horn, and all the men ran towards the boats. The other day at Lajes, the funeral cortege for a whaler killed at sea was setting off when a whale was sighted from Gallows Hill. Everyone was grief-stricken—the widow was grief-stricken, the fishermen were full of grief, the priest, the sacristan, the cross, and the vessel of holy water—those rough, grimy men were advancing solemnly and dressed in their best suits—and then the slow rhythm of the march came to a sudden halt and their mood changed immediately: the priest was left by himself, stuttering his Latin, the coffin lying in the middle of the street, while the rest, in a throng, and taking the sacristan with them, rushed toward the beach. Whale! Whale! . . . They will leave a wedding celebration or a funeral halfway through, a contract or a financial deal, witness or judicial obligations, and rush off with all urgency to join a whale hunt. At Cais do Pico and Lajes, no one strays far from the beach. They are always waiting for the signal, their ears ever alert, the men in the fields, the women in the hovels. And while they talk, eat, or work, deep down, they all have the same nagging concern. They are so wrapped up in the activity that even this awful, nauseous stink, which works its way into food and clothing, smells good to them.

"Whale! Whale ahoy!"

And the entire population makes for the boats. From here, I have a view of the row of houses along the side of the road, the wharf with the grease-covered wooden warehouse, black, smoky, and fetid, and everywhere, on the slippery rocks and in the blue water, vertebrae, carcasses bobbing around, and bloody remains that smell of putrefaction and reek to high heaven.

"May Our Lord go with them!"

"Lord deliver it to them and keep them safe from peril!" the women say.

"That boat is my José's bread and butter," another woman shouts, pushing towards the men who are hurriedly hauling the boat into the water.

"And isn't that boat there going to set off?"

"It's waiting for the harpooner."

By now, a group of older men, their hands shielding their eyes, are peering out over the water, to see if they can catch sight of the plumes of vapor expelled from the creature's blowhole.

The sea fades, more ethereal than the sky, while the gold of the clouds gradually dissolves into the azure. A diffuse light flickers on the quivering surface. It is an exquisite morning—a stretch of light-blue sky that cannot be distinguished from the light-blue sea. In the background, sparse wisps of vapor; on the right, puffs of flaky white over São Jorge; and further out to sea, thick pulpy formations hang still in the morning light. Over there, a shred of mist has become entangled in the almost-gray waters, and does not let go:

in the distance, Faial is a glassy smudge, and Pico parades before my eyes in different gradations, from newborn blue to violet. Mist sticks to the black pebbles, the awe-inspiring hills, or suddenly melts into the waters in passing showers. In the sky, there is such a clear blue that one can barely distinguish it, a blue amid longer patches of blue, with lighter interstices, and then, straight above these, thin layers on top of each other . . . But all of this is opaque; all of this is seen through a light, receding mist. It is a morning on which to breathe slowly. The sea is still mist, the sky is all mist; there is only some blue mixed with the white and some light filtered through the clouds . . .

The whaleboat hovers as if in midair, while others go on ahead under the power of their oars. Two have hoisted their sails . . . One of these boats is almost like a piece of furniture that is at once elegant and resistant, very well built with light cedar planks, nailed with bronze bolts onto ribs of American oak—as slim as a fish and as light as a shell, for slipping over the waters. There is a crew of seven men, the harpoon and lance to attack a creature with a body mass that may be in the region of a hundred tons and which, once it has been injured, sometimes turns against the whaleboats or even against a ship of its own size. Only a week ago, a sperm whale reduced a boat to splinters and killed three men, rearing up out of the sea, its gaping mouth full of baleen.[16] It is important to bear in mind that the whale is a very timid creature. It may cover and smother a whaleboat with the fan of its tail—and yet

---

[16] Most whales have no teeth—sperm whales have teeth in the lower jaw. Most whales live in polar waters and sperm whales in warm waters, where they seek out craggy rocks (author's note).

everything scares it. Few whales go on the attack, even when
they have been wounded; but there are lone males that have
even dared to attack ships bigger than themselves, sinking
them with a single head-charge. Older whales become isolated as they find it hard to get enough food: they chew up
the sea never-endingly, like oxen grazing grass. The young
whales travel in groups of twenty or thirty. To encounter a
pod of whales in the morning, exhaling through their blowholes, is a majestic sight—it is a sight from the very begin-
nings of the world . . . A light mist—blue sea! . . . There they
go, their backs arching out of the water, occasionally releasing a jet of vaporized water into the air. Then, suddenly, they
almost simultaneously show their tails and dive, emerging
further ahead, water running off their gleaming backs . . . It
is a heart-stopping sight, a vast picture, and one of excep-
tional vigor.

They feed. They always follow the same route seeking out
the gelatinous flesh they live on; these include cephalopods
such as squid and octopus, which they catch and suck in amid
arms that wind themselves around and lash them, an ever-
chewed whitened mass dribbling from their mouths. They
are the great devourers of monsters that await their prey in
the blue-green water like bags topped with horrible, soft tentacles, moving around their beak like some reptilian crown.

Alone or in pods, they follow their route to Africa, returning the same way. The whalers wait for them and hunt
them, to such an extent that they are scarce in the waters
of the archipelago, and have only begun to reappear after
the Americans abandoned whaling, and oil from minerals
began to replace whale oil, which is nowadays used only in
precision instruments. In recent times, a large number of
sperm whales have returned to the Azores: on one day alone,
I saw five in the bay of Porto Pim, on Faial, five grayish-blue
animals, with short, thick fins, and horizontal flukes split

in the middle like a swallow's tail. I watched those massive, unusual monsters, with rectangular heads that take up a third of the body, and where there is nothing that can be taken for use. In a whale, it is not the belly that is the largest, most voluminous part of the creature—it is the head; from there the body grows rounder and tapers right down to the tail, horizontal, enormous, and glistening. As for the eyes, you have to look for them carefully, because they are barely distinguishable from the skin, and, sadly for them, they are placed in such a way that they can only see what is on either side of them. The whalers approach them easily from their tail end—it is a question of not making any noise—for they possess very acute hearing, and an ability to hear through their skin: they can sense things from a great distance: any unusual sound troubles them, causing them to quiver with fright until they remember to swim away. At the front of their head are their two blowholes: it is impossible for a harpoon to penetrate at this point because the skin is very hard; and underneath, their jaws open in the form of a spout with large teeth, which, when they close their mouth, enter cavities in the upper jawbone.

This innocent, stupid creature is almost always asleep or digesting on the surface of the water, inert like a full sack . . . Only after I saw its head being cut open, like a shapeless black watermelon, but pinkish-white inside, did I begin to understand the whale. I fruitlessly sought a brain. Instead of a brain, it has a liquid, spermaceti, which provides twelve to fifteen barrels of the best oil. Nor is there any need to boil it: it is ready for use in fuel tanks. That is why it allows itself to be caught . . .

Whalers know straightaway whether it is large or small from the time it spends on the surface of the water; the species it belongs to, because some only breathe through one blowhole. They know when it is about to dive, because they first wave their flukes in the air; and whether they are calves, because these swim and jump in groups, such is their agility. They say that a mother accompanied by her calf, which is four or five meters long when it is born, is easier to subjugate, and the *ambaque,* or black whale, even allows itself to be killed when her offspring is caught: it is enough to wound it near its tail and haul it over alongside the boat. The mother will not abandon it and, if she cannot escape with it under her fin, prefers to die under the thrusts of the whaler's lance. In other words, this monstrous blue-gray creature, with a head full of oil, does not only eat and digest, sleep and digest—it is capable of tenderness and self-sacrifice.

I think it is only in the Azores that whales are still hunted using these primitive, very dangerous methods. The Americans use a special cannon and, until relatively recently, large numbers of whaling ships would leave the coasts of America for long periods of time, sailing down to northern Chile or the polar seas, where whales find their nutrients in waters full of sustenance, minute organisms in formation like nebulae. The whale is caught, hung up, cut, and boiled down in huge smoking cauldrons on board ship. This grease-smeared monstrosity, reeking and dripping oil, sails on all day long, vomiting smoke and a paralyzing smell, and seems more like a traveling butchery than it does a ship. Everything inside it is sticky and slippery. Great hooks hoist the pieces of whale, depositing them in the cauldrons, where they boil over and over again. Around these, men toil, greased to their souls, among flames, a band of adventurers, a motley crew, Malays and Chinese, as slippery as the ship, this old crab that haunts any sea where a whale can be found. At the top of the masts, in two barrels, the lookouts constantly scan the waters through their glasses, while others repeatedly stir the cauldrons or, on boards lashed to the hull, cut, hoist, and hack the beast's blubber to pieces.

And this is never-ending: the ship fills the sea with stench and blood, while inside it the mass of flesh is ceaselessly rendered, plunged in thick smoke that remains undispersed by the wind—it cannot be dispersed—while it goes on hunting, goes on killing, as if its mission were to sully the ocean's great purity. The thick, heavy smoke envelops the bloodstained ship, which stands out in the gentle morning air or in the gold-tinged sunset. And even at night, under the beauty of a starry sky, the ship is ruddy and ablaze, burning flesh and forever belching smoke. And the stink grows ever stronger . . .

The sea is gray with smooth patches where the gray-gold reflects the color of the clouds, and, in the background, almost touching the sky, there is a huge blue expanse . . . The pod of whales emerges from under there in a blue that is blue combined with action. They all emerge from the icy ocean as if they were coming from the source of life itself. And they feel the unconscious freshness of joy that surrounds them, the blue water born in surge upon surge, communicating its energy to them so that they all quiver in response to it. They have no art, no philosophy, nor business dealings. They live through their skin, they live through the water that is alive all around them. They cut through the great sea, leaping in unison, on mist-filled mornings, on golden evenings, huge as the universe and all of them golden, on stormy days, made for them to dance across the surface of the waves, piercing the lively white swell—with another swell in the distance—or on afternoons when the sea is calm, made for them to float and sleep, in the ocean and the world together all blue, and which also sleeps and reposes. A creature floats on its own. It is sleeping or digesting. It looks like a dark rock on the surface of the waters . . . A sigh! We are in the first hours of life. The clarity is reflected and runs along the animal's sleek, dark spine. The boat approaches soundlessly, the harpooner in the prow, his harpoon raised and gripped firmly in both his hands, his feet steady, standing ready for the thrust. It has a metal barb seventy-five centimeters in length and a handle two meters long. Next to him in the boat is the lance, which is bigger, and will finish off this monster the size of a building. But I am more struck by the man than by the whale: he is formidable, standing there, minute, all life concentrated in his eyes and his hands. On the boat, everyone is silent and tense, no one utters an unnecessary word: men, boat, harpooner, and harpoon, all are possessed of the same body and the same soul. There are seven of them, all in the grip of the action, permeated by the air and by this smell that penetrates the mouth and the pores of the skin, a generator of energy—it is one united living being, consisting only of nerves and willpower, hunting a monster and with a touch of danger to lend it additional attraction—not to mention the potential for making money, which is excellent. All of them profit from it: a whale provides a lot of oil, and oil brings in a lot of money. Sometimes it provides ambergris. But it is mainly the need to kill, to struggle (in a life that is more monotonous than anywhere else—doubly monotonous because of the sea that encircles them and the hills that wall them in), to overcome adversity and danger—feelings that are rooted in the deepest recesses of the human soul.

There are seven leathery, determined crew, some of them white haired, their faces etched with lines, and the harpooner ready to release the steel spring, focusing all his energy in his gaze and in his muscles. They wait—he for the moment when he will fire the harpoon, the others to pull the boat away at that precise moment. It is a moment like no other.

By now, other boats are approaching . . . But before they can take the whale themselves, the harpooner launches his weapon. There is a moment of hesitation and shock from the creature, like the bull when they plant the banderillas in him, and this allows the boat to swerve away with a pull of the oars, before it gets flattened by the flukes or caught in the ensuing whirlpool. There is not so much as a second of doubt or one false move. The whale plunges into the waves, and there is a risk that it will drag them to the bottom or carry them at the speed of an express train out into the open seas, because that huge mass is astoundingly agile. "Let it out! Let it out! Let the rope out! . . ." And forward they go in the animal's troughed wake of water ripped violently apart, keeping a close eye on the line.

The other whaleboats are left with nothing. Sometimes there is a squabble: all the boats want to catch the same whale and make for its tail, its head, its flanks; they have even, on occasion, fallen blindly on the animal, landing on its back and harpooning its head. On other occasions, an impatient harpooner, seeing his prey escape, has thrown his lance onto the boat nearest to the whale in order to steal it. This is what they call short-cut harpooning.

"Let it out! Let it out!"

The whale has dipped. The hemp line, which has been neatly coiled in two tubs, is now paying out, and the men, ashen-faced and motionless, their hearts constrained, wait. The whale may disappear for twenty minutes. One of the crew holds a cloth called a *nepa* so that the hemp will not cut his hands as he pays it out through the *moirão*, a wooden chock on the boat's bow, which sometimes even smokes with the friction. Sometimes the line runs out if the whale goes down very deep. If there is another boat nearby, they will provide more line, otherwise the whale will be lost: they have to slash the hemp or they will be dragged into the abyss.

"There goes the ark!" they exclaim.

The ark is the end of the line, and they are reluctant to see it go. They pass the tip round from hand to hand, until the last crew member, who tosses it away in despair.

"There goes the ark!"

Worse still is when the injured whale throws itself against the boat. It tears it to pieces with its mouth, then turns to the men, its mouth wide open like some wild beast. The other day, the boats that had witnessed this drama tried to lance the infuriated creature, but the others yelled from the water as they swam:

"Hey, there! Stay away, otherwise it'll kill us all!"

In most cases, the whale dives down, and then resurfaces before the line runs out, and it shows its snout first so that it can exhale. This is when they approach and stab it with the lance next to the flipper in order to draw blood. It dips, resurfaces, and they wear it down, knowing they have it when blood begins to spurt from its blowhole. What expression of alarm then appears inside the creature's huge head? There are whales that manage to escape but never forget—throwing themselves at the whalers months later. These give it more thrusts with their lance, shouting triumphantly, "It's ours! It's ours!" Crimson gushes from its body, its heart, its lungs. It vomits. The men are sprayed red. Then, that great body lurches, keels over, and dies in a thickening pool of blood . . .

From the top of the hill, the lookout has guided the whaleboat, with beacons lit for the smoke to direct it—to starboard, port, out to sea—until they find the animal, and the entire population has watched the spectacle nervously.

"They've furled the sails!"

"The whale's harpooned! The whale's harpooned!"

"It was Master Francisco who harpooned the whale."

"Hey, if it was my man who harpooned the whale, today is Saint Peter's Day!"

And the cry is relayed from house to house throughout the village.

"The whale's harpooned!"

The worst part is to come; the animal needs to be brought back to dry land, which can take hours, sometimes the whole day. Sometimes the boats are dragged far away and the whale has to be towed back to the coast. And the rest follows: they need to cut it up, cut the surface blubber into pieces to boil them up in the cauldrons. The boat is stowed, the twisted harpoon taken to the smithy. The quays are slathered with grease and slippery; the shed emits a sticky, fetid smoke; rotting pieces of carcass float on the sea; everywhere, there are whale bones and shapeless entrails. From inside the hellish kitchen come blasts, flashes, and smoke. Entire villages stink of fat, for even the fire under the cauldrons is fed with the vertebrae and skins of the whale. One passes by and sees a huge head split open with an axe, or a monster laid out with men on top of it cutting it with a long iron blade tied to a pole, while others, covered in grease and blood, rummage around in the intestines, where they sometimes come across a fortune. From one that I saw lying dead at Cais do Pico, they had taken thirty kilos of dark mass, ambergris, which was worth many thousands of *réis*. Everywhere, there are wax-filled basins, barrels of oil, great piles of bones, residues of firewood, and white fat cut into pieces. A crane hoists an enormous chunk of whale out of the water. There is yet more smell, more smoke, in that hellish butchery. More stench . . . One can hardly distinguish the men at the back of this repugnant shed, stirring the cauldrons with huge spoons, while others carry sheets of blubber dripping with grease. Red and blue flashes (it is the oil burning and the flesh sizzling) light up these strange figures. Even the sea is scarlet.

Green and black, green and gray, amid charred whale rinds. A titanic existence full of mists, vague, sparse flashes, delicate tints melding into one another, and from time to time a piece of blue-gray sea that grips and fascinates me. But what I can never forget is the fat chunk of flesh, the rancid stench that never leaves my nose, or that grease-laden ship journeying over the sea, leaving in its wake traces of smoke and blood . . .

Men and Boats

The men are pillars of rectitude. It is not only on Corvo that there are no crimes—crimes are rare on the other islands as well. Perhaps this is because of isolation. "Put a train service," people say, "linking the islands with the mainland, and you'll see how crimes are committed every day. There are no crimes because the criminals cannot get away." It is not like that. The men of Pico are among the most morally robust men I have met. They stand before me like towers, and a look in the eye that does not deceive. And the men of Flores and Corvo? . . . Maybe it is their race, their simple, isolated existence, their work, and the permanent contact with soil and sea. From what I could surmise, they greatly cherish their independence. They emigrate in order to buy one or two fields and they end up as farmers. Almost all the folk on Corvo and Faial can read. There is less illiteracy than on the mainland. Look at the countryfolk, the neatness of their homes and the situation of women, who are treated with respect and tenderness. Some women work on the land, but almost all of them do needlework. How many times, on

market days, have I seen this depressing sight on the roads
(Leiria, etc.): the man on horseback and next to him, the poor
woman, barefoot, her little steps keeping up with the animal
as it trots along! . . . She has given him his life and his children, and gazes upon him with love. This is just not possible
in the Azores: it is another race, either that or has respect for
the woman come from America, to where almost all of them
emigrate?

Some of these men are quite extraordinary characters, the
whalers of Corvo, for example, half a dozen old men who
still survive, at once childlike and dignified, their grey goa-
tees combed out like fans on their otherwise cleanshaven
faces. They look like brothers; they speak with gravity. They
express both innocence and pain. The whaling ships came for
them at Corvo and Flores and took them away for long years
at a time or forever . . .

Banzeca (on Flores) is a jolly, toothless old man, with a
mischievous glint in his eyes, set in a weasel's face, who spent
his life traveling the oceans, only to end up back on dry land,
with a yearning for dangers past. He is a character with salt
on his tongue like the waters of the sea.

"I was always a fisherman, a *terraço*, and whatever I earned
paid for my food. My life in America, where I went as a boy,
was always spent in cod fishing . . . We set off in April for the
banks in a schooner with a captain and a cook, five dories,
and two men for each dory, the devil of a mixture, blacks,
Chinese, Portuguese, and goodness know what else—the
world! . . . Only the captain is American. The ship carries salt,
bait, and supplies, but you need an iron belly to survive in it.
It smells of all that is bad—cod and rottenness, and it sticks to
you like oil. With a sparse wind, it takes six days to reach the
sea of fog from America. And you don't see anything apart
from fog, fog, and more fog . . . Sometimes the fog lifts like
smoke and a white island appears, an island of snow moving

through the sea and heading straight for us. The ships drop anchor five miles from each other, schooners, barques, boats, all with their topmasts stowed because of the bad weather, which sometimes fills you with fear. Then the fishing begins. We get up at three in the morning (there, it doesn't matter whether it's day or night, it's all the same) and, after we eat, the dories are gotten ready for fishing, two men in each, and they go wherever the fish is biting. If there's nothing, they weigh anchor and try somewhere else. At midday on clear days, the ship hoists a rag at the top of its mast and others ring a bell—that's the call for dinner. Then, after dinner, we go back to fishing again, standing in the boat, two lines in each hand, sou'wester on our head, oilskin jackets and trousers, and big boots on our feet—always over the fishing banks and the boats not far from each other. Sometimes folk talk from one boat to another, but they're always hard at work. We go on working until midnight, and those returning from fishing sleep like a log straightaway, until three in the morning, when the captain shouts, "Everyone up!" They all work, those fishing and those on board; green boys (those at sea for the first time) do the scaling, and they scale away nonstop, big knives in their hands, cutting the heads off the fish, slitting them, passing them on to the next person, who guts them and separates the liver. Then another throws the fish through the hatch into the hold, where it's salted and packed in barrels. The only rest day is Sunday. And no one ever falls ill . . . Their hands burn because of the fishing lines and from the saltwater, they are damp from top to bottom, the smell sticks to their body and to their soul—but everything runs smoothly: they eat like horses, they've got bellies of iron."

He talked about his life on the Grand Banks for hours and I saw the thick fog over the calm sea, the little boats lost in the gloom, feeling their way along with the help of the ship's siren, and those eerie mists that come from the North

Pole. And I felt the dampness permeating clothes and bodies, in those ships that smell of brine and the steam emanating from clothes drying out next to the stoves. I bore witness to their monotonous existence in the isolation of the sea; the return of the boats emptying the fish onto the deck, until the commotion increases and they all wash, scale, and salt the fish through the night, until there is no salt left and the schooner is full. Miraculous feats of fishing sometimes, catches in which only two lines uncoiled from the tubs—cast into the seas and pulled in at night—manage to fill three *douros,* which is the name given to these little craft.

"And what about the crew? Was it good?"

"On the ships I crewed, they were almost all Portuguese, except for the captain and pilot. Sometimes, while we were fishing out in the boats, we would gossip and joke about the girls back home, things that had happened in the Azores, and we would even sometimes talk about that cod ship which had been sunk by another one, killing everyone, and which can sometimes be seen through the mists for a moment, with its company still fishing and fulfilling their destiny. We were scared . . . they're stories people tell. Other times, we'd watch the fog turn into a living thing, into tiny birds, thousands of them, their little wings flapping through that endless cool air, screeching between the patches of mist. At night, the shearwaters talk among themselves. Even in the thickest of the gloom, these creatures are feverish with joy. Especially some black birds the size of starlings, that fly about, screeching, they flutter around folk screeching like hell, so many of them, as abundant as the sands in the sea, and we call them *alminhas do mestre,* or the master's little souls."

Others, such as the lad from Pico, a stout-hearted boy, tall, weather-beaten, and merry, who went to America when he was seventeen, go to fish mackerel and only return home to get married. It is always the same life. He sailed on a schooner, fished for days on end with nets off the coast of America. The mackerel is filleted, salted, and packed in barrels. Sometimes it is taken to Boston and sold fresh.

"A brother of mine went with me, and he's still there on the Grand Banks. He worked for four years on whaling ships and is coming home to get married."

It is this man who tells me stories of an extraordinary sea, a sea that is both water and food, a sea that is like milk, sustaining shoals of fish, ships so packed together they all but form a compact mat, upon which thousands of birds feed, filling the darkness with the pulsating of wings and cries.

Many men have spent their whole lives at sea and have no knowledge of the world outside. It is even hard to understand what they are saying. An old whaler on Corvo insisted on telling me of some great dramatic event—something that had been the most interesting episode in his existence—but that I never got to understand, because it had neither beginning nor end:

"We were fishing for fresh mackerel. We had the lamps lit and were getting ready to haul the fish in, when a ship bore down on us, hit our bows, and dragged our anchor. It snapped our boom. So we went over to detach our anchor and get out of the way . . . Then we saw another ship on our bow that turned away in another direction. We were low on food stocks. We hoisted a flag at half-mast, but the barque . . ."

"What barque?"

"The French barque ignored us and continued on its course . . ."

"Oh! . . ."

He stopped talking and I looked at him, and he, his candid eyes full of enthusiasm, happily gazing at me.

"Oh, of course! . . ."

Almost all the men, and even the women, emigrate to America, and for those who do not emigrate, it is because they cannot escape. If America were to open its doors wide, the Azores would become depopulated. As it is, there is a shortage of manpower for agricultural work in the islands . . . There are some who become market gardeners in Bermuda, like this old man who is returning there and sails with me on the same liner, the Britannia, and who tells me about his life, resting on his haunches, which is how people work in his profession, in order to sketch on the deck with the tip of his finger the beds he grows for onions, parsley, and Savoy cabbage, with which he supplies the market in New York.

What a host of images I carry in my mind! I see before me the port of New York almost a century ago—the port for all the desperadoes and the ideologues, the port for emigrants from all corners of the world. America! Day and night, boats unloading human cargoes. Through the eyes of these emigrants, I see a ranch, a life of freedom galloping across the endless plain, and scenes that no longer exist: the hallucinating sight of fire preparing the land to receive its first seeds. Nearby flows the great virgin river, swollen and in flood, as yet without well-defined limits. As in the first days of the Creation—and next to it stands the rustic farmhouse, defended by its wall of thick blackened tree trunks. Another tells me of multitudes of adventurers, whalers who have jumped ship, hustlers and bandits all advancing—and the baggage trains crossing thousands of miles, and those who arrive by sea after journeying across plains, savannas, deserts dotted with candelabra cactuses, as if the uninhabited world had no end. This same witness gave me descriptions of the first rice and indigo plantations on the banks of the Sacramento, and, from the mouth of Petinga, who is a hundred years old, reduced to skin and bone, but who still has a glint in his eye, I managed to get a glimpse of the gold rush to California in 1841, when San Francisco shook to its foundations, cities expanded exponentially, and, from all parts of the world, the rabble set off and descended upon America. Gold! . . . The human whirlwind headed to the country's ports from New England, or prepared to cross the continent. From all points of the globe, multitudes set sail for the promised land of gold. From one day to the next, San Francisco became one of the world's major cities. To get rich, all one had to do was to set off, having bought a pan and a basket to sift the sand. Everything became jumbled in my memory, the individual scenes and the giant canvasses, as the emigrants told me of their harsh, adventurous lives . . .

It is a pleasure to talk to them when they are quick and alert. Nearly all of them have a story to tell, because almost all of them traveled the world in order to get away from military service. They are retired sailors, such as old Captain Fidalgo from Lajes, who, at the age of eighty, sitting by his little window, cannot take his eyes off the waters, his yearnings ever greater, and who, he says, will die with his gaze fixed on the sea; there is a mariner, as tall and weathered as a beam, who is growing old in his rocky plot of land he bought with American dollars, and which he tends with extreme care, his garden as neat and pristine as a ship's deck. One of them tells me that, at the age of seven, he was bathing on a beach at Horta when an American whaler that had called in for supplies grabbed him and took him aboard. No one saw the incident. His mother wept, and the family assumed he had been eaten by a great white or a cow shark. He lived there for many years, only returning to Faial when he was twenty, by which time he no longer spoke Portuguese, or knew anyone. One or two vague memories led him to his home. No one knew who he was. Others had vanished into the huge wide world:

"One time I was the quartermaster on a ship that visited the island of Príncipe. I noticed a little chapel high up on a hill. The bell, which was hanging on the branch of an orange tree began to ring. 'Let's go ashore . . .' I landed and climbed the hill. I was talking to the priest, when I saw a man with a long beard whom I recognized from his look. 'Is that you, João?' It was someone who had left Faial many years before. 'That's me.' 'Come back home with me on the ship. Everyone thinks you're dead.' 'Not a chance of that! Here, I've got food and drink. I'm married to a dumb black woman, but I have all I need. If I went back to Faial I'd have to work in order to eat.' And there was no way of persuading him. He gave me a hug and there he stayed. We never met each other again."

Others were involved in whaling and visited the islands of Fiji to take on water. There is a large concave bay with a range of red mountains at the back and coconut palms, casuarinas, and acacias along the seashore. Every so often, there are dense downfalls of rain which cause the huge thick flowers to let out a strong perfume like a last sigh. The nights are full of languor and peace. The smell of the pandan makes you dizzy. Everyone is overcome with apathy in that tropical climate. The king sent women aboard for them, as many women as they wanted, big, strong, copper-colored women, who danced in groups performing rituals connected with fishing, sowing, the harvest, or little scenes of life on the land or the sea, and would end up surrendering to the men open-lipped and voluptuous. They stayed there for nearly a month. Each man had three, four, or five women. Despite the captain's angry warnings, it proved impossible to drag them away from the place. When, at long last, they had to leave, the men were so tired they were unable to hoist the sails and the women burst out into sobbing laments on the shore . . .

At Lajes, I met Experiente, a curious character who builds skiffs and is in competition with another fellow to see who

builds the best and safest ones and, at Madalena, the extraordinary Chatinha family, the son, a heroic fisherman in the face
of the eternal force of nature, who tells of his roaming on
the sea, and the father, a ring in his ear, like all the old sailors,
wizened, his face dry and cleanshaven like a herring—when
he laughs his face wrinkles into hieroglyphics—married to
Aunty Anica, who is an excellent cook of all manner of fish.
Master Chatinha is a fisherman and a philosopher:

"In life, we should always play safe. Take me, I never do
anything without first consulting my wife. I always listen to
that good woman. The other day, I had to build a boat, and
I couldn't make up my mind, so I went and asked her: 'Hey,
woman, should I build a sailboat or a skiff?'

"'Do whatever you want.'

"'I know that! But I just want your opinion.'

"'I don't understand anything about these things.'

"'But answer my question: shall I build a sailboat or a skiff?'

"'Well, seeing as you're so insistent, I think you should
make a skiff.'

"Well, obviously, I built a sailboat. Because we should
always consult our women—so as to do the opposite of what
they say."

On Flores, deep-sea fishing is extraordinarily fruitful, and is
almost always done by using a line or a fishing rod. They take
the fish they catch home, or exchange it for corn. On both
Flores and Corvo, the tackle they use includes the single hook
line, multihook line, dropline, tangle net, troll line, landing
net, and the cast net, just as they do in almost all the islands.
The vast majority of the fishing industry involves whaling,
with the exception of São Miguel, where there is a whole
quarter made up of cod fishermen and a number of villages,

among these Mosteiro, with a jagged hillside behind, clusters of little houses and mills working by the seashore—folk
employed exclusively in deep-sea fishing. They use a net for
jack mackerel, line and rod out as far as the sea of Ferraria,
Matoso, Ponta da Bretanha, and they sell the fish in the nearest villages. For the Pico fishermen, the best waters are the
Princesa bank, but there is also the São Mateus shoal, the São
Jorge sandbar, the Velho, Novo, and Fora seas, where the fish
are plentiful. Prior to the discovery by the Prince of Monaco
observatory,[17] the sea that provided the greatest abundance of
fish was the stretch between Ponta Negra and Ponta do Hos-
pital. Bogues are caught using a landing net; mackerel with a
rod and single hook line; bluefish, golden bream, and amberjack with a rod and big hooks. Bait is prepared by rolling the
fish in cinders and pricking it with the tip of a knife. On Terceira, there are also two major villages for deep-sea fishing,
Praia da Vitória and São Mateus, some cottages and a harbor
formed by volcanic rocks. They carry out line fishing in boats
that take five or six crew, for conger, forkbeard, moray, lob-
ster, mackerel with a smaller hook, and sardines with what is
called a purse-seine net, and which is dragged landward until
the fish is drawn under the lines. They go out to the Nordeste
and Prata seas, Cabeço de Esquiola, Baixio, Aregos, Palheiros,
Invés, and to the Novo sea, leaving at midnight and getting
out to a depth of 150 feet and sometimes, as in the case of the
Cacete waters, 500 feet. There are thirty boats. The men take
a bag of bread, a pitcher of water, and fish by way of supplies.
Occasionally, sea conditions force them to make for Biscoitos,
as the ginger-haired, sunburnt fellow explains when I ask him:

"How do you know where you are when you're at sea?"

---

[17] The "Observatório Príncipe Alberto de Mónaco", situated on the island
of Faial, is a meteorological and oceanographic institute, which was estab-
lished at the beginning of the 20th century (translator's note).

"If we're northeast and land is beginning to get faint, we know where we are by the waves, because once we're outside the Queimado, the waves are always the same, even with a wind blowing . . ."

"But what happens in bad weather?"

"If the new wave undoes the old one, then we're done for," which means the storm is going to be so strong that the boat will be unable to withstand it.

I have never seen so many or such beautiful fish. Throughout the archipelago, they catch red scorpionfish, darkly spotted with large elegant side fins like wings, the magnificent forkbeard of two varieties, the black coastal type and the other, which is greenish in color, bluntnose shark, albacore tuna, Ballan wrasse, bonito, red sea bream, yellowmouth barracuda, blackbelly rosefish, jack mackerel, common mackerel, conger, golden bream, bluefish, white trevally, blackspot sea bream, blacktail comber, amberjack, grey mullet, moray, sand smelt, common sea bream, Spanish serra mackerel, sardine, sargo, trumpetfish, etc. The Princesa Alice bank alone would provide enough to feed an empire.

Reapers of the sea and reapers of the land, for almost all of them cultivate a patch of soil and harvest fish to eat. If the fishermen emigrate on whaling ships, the farmers go and work on the ranches of America.

Almost all of them are happy, almost all cultivate a piece of land that belongs to them. The islanders on Graciosa export corn and work hard, sustaining themselves well among their fields and vines, refusing to allow themselves to be abused. Years ago, when a landlord in Lisbon attempted to increase their rents, they refused to pay. Soldiers were sent—they only paid what was fair. I have never seen such well-tended fields between the two hills with the white village in the middle, one of the hills covered in flowering broom, the other such a gentle green in hue that it seems to flow down the slopes. It is an illustrious literary island. Chateaubriand talks of it in his *Memoirs from beyond the Tomb* and in his *Essai sur les révolutions*, and Garret lived in one of the cottages there at the time of Dom Pedro's expedition. On São Jorge, the tragic island, it is worth listening to the voice of the cowherd, the quiet complaint of the most unfortunate man in the Azores. On this island of large landowners, who rent out their pastures for a certain number of *canadas*[18] of milk, there are places that pay every year five hundred *canadas* of milk per cow and others less. The cowherds take their milk to the dairy, where it is turned into butter, and at the end of the year, they pay the landlord in cash. The higher the price of milk, the worse it is for the cowherd, whose rent is based on a fixed number of *canadas*. They live in villages and every morning and evening they go out to the fields to milk their cows.

This fellow talking to me is dark-skinned and huge, his hair in a ponytail, a bonnet with ear flaps, and a knee-length cape.

"How is your lordship and his obligations (meaning his family)?"

I pause in front of this primitive figure and ask after his wife.

"She is half spent, on account of having some family a few days ago (she had a baby)."

He is waiting for one of his sons to go and fetch water for the cattle:

"As (when) he comes . . ."

---

[18] An old measurement for liquids corresponding to about two liters (translator's note).

Every day, he has to carry water, sometimes from a long way off, to give the animals to drink; every day, along with his wife and children, he goes milking, after which he takes it to the dairy.

He is a sad, lonely, forlorn figure in that woebegone wasteland. The whole island, ever since I first saw it, struck me as wretched . . . He explains to me that when the cows are in full milk, they have to be milked twice a day; later, towards the end of July, there is not enough pasture left, and the animals start producing less milk. So they take them back to Rocha, where they spend the winter with them, so that the pastures can recover and produce better grazing in the summer. All soaked through, or as they put it, "under the weather," they wait for the rainy season to pass before starting the same monotonous routine again. These abandoned, poverty-stricken men possess a certain mystery to them in their isolation and exploitation.

I notice with amazement that this cowherd is telling me about his life with complete indifference, planted before me like a tree trunk. He is brutish, but it was others who reduced him to this brutish condition. The bleakest things, he talks about with the same blank expression. Isolation has muted him, and the harshness of the heather has covered him with gloom. He has been washed by the wind and rain.

I should add that the island is mesmerizing and only half an island, sliced through vertically, all blackened rock on one side. It is all length, and has a sinister look about it. They had already told me about its wild cowherds, its fathers of their own grandchildren, wrapped in their capes and living in promiscuity, and I gazed at that cliff face without a blemish on it as if it concealed a secret . . .

A forbidding island, except, perhaps, for the northern side, which is more rustic: from Urzelina to the Costa do Rosário, it is all rock; on the southern side, from Urzelina

to the Ponta dos Rosais, unbroken stone; and in the interior, monotonous rolling landscape. We climb to the top of
one crest and another appears in front of us, divided into
fields by heather that is almost black in color. Pastures, pastures . . . Mournful land, an impression of harshness. From
the top of the Terreiro da Marcela, we glimpse the sea full of
nebulousness, blue tones, vague flashes of light dancing on
the surface of the waters, great unlimited spaces, and, under
a gray, overcast sky, we fancy we can make out Terceira in
the distance, lost in the mist, with Pico in front of us and
Graciosa, unsure, like some apparition that is about to take
on concrete shape. I descend and continue along the road
around the island: by now, there is a streak of intense crimson between the clouds on the horizon. From one lookout
spot known as the Miradouro, I catch sight of a wide area
of fertile and cultivated flat terrain next to the sea, which
stretches as far as Urzelina, and the village between the
Morro and the Pico dos Loiros, with its little circular harbor.
I am told about the picturesque northern side, but I have lost
interest in everything since I met the cowherd. All I can hear
is his slavish tone of voice . . .

"We spend our life going hither and thither . . . Most of
our time's spent carrying water for the animals."

"And the milk?"

"Let me tell you . . . The milk is for the landlord, and if
the cows don't produce any, we have to pay the same, and
at whatever price the dairy wants to set. What's left for the
cowherd, who lives with his family in a *rautilha* (little old cottage), are a few calves that are hard to rear, because we need
to take the mother's milk to the dairy. What happens is sometimes these calves die—so help me, God! And sometimes, at
the end of the year, to make ends meet, we have to sell a
cow to pay the rent. We never, never earn enough to pay the
landlord. We've got to a point where we can't live like this!"

I have never been confronted by such an impassive figure.
It was not isolation that made him so: more than abandonment, it was scorn for a fellow human being that created
him. One's feelings towards this earthbound creature do
not involve pity, but fear, as if for the first time I have come
face to face with another type of man, more akin to animals
than to his fellow men. No one comes close to this slave in
the solitude of the sea and pasture. What I feel is a desire
to escape out of fear that this may be contagious. There he
remains, abandoned like an animal, and I look back at him
from afar, standing motionless as if he were made of stone—
there where pain does not enter, and, if it does, it immediately turns to stone.

Where you live at close quarters with the people is on the
ferries that ply between the islands. To cross the channel
between Corvo and Flores, I climb aboard an old sailing boat
of worn deck planks and triangular sails, held by two ropes,
one at the prow, which is called a *burro* (donkey), the other,
the mainsail is controlled by the captain. To hoist the sail,
the men grab the *urraca* (gaff), pulling it until the master
suddenly shouts, because of the wind, "Top the yards! Top
the yards!" so that they can cross the yard, which they call
the "pole." And off we sail in the old crab . . . The crossing
can take anything between three and eleven hours, depending on the wind, the waters, the sudden gusts that occur in
mid-channel, almost always aggravated by the Gulf Stream.
At the bottom of the boat I notice a lance, lying there casu-
ally, and I ask what it is for: "To kill sharks, sometimes they
leap aboard." Then I crouch in a corner next to a clutch of
women, sacks, two pigs, a young heifer with its legs tied, a
large crate, and a crowd of people who have taken advantage

of the occasion to take a ride over to Flores. But I cannot take my eyes off the sea. It is the custom, halfway across the channel, with the sail full, for the sailors to doff their hats and say prayers to Our Lady. The prayers take some time, and give us an opportunity to observe their solemn faces, where life has left its imprint, the faces of the older men dry and wrinkled like little old apples. The boat's master, Hilário, has a weather-beaten face, with dark, alert eyes; the captain's eyes are blue and his complexion ruddy, as he watches the high waves and directs maneuvers; the faces of the young girls, innocent as animals, huddled together. "Our Father for the dead!" This is the last prayer. "Our Father for those who have died in this channel!" "Our Father so that the Lord may take us safely to port!" I pray as well, with one eye on the lance and another on this old wreck with its loosening planks, loaded to the gunnels with people: "For the souls of those who have died in this channel—for my soul!" . . . But by now the contours of the island of Flores are coming into focus, with its tall black pinnacles. The sea is violet, the island green, and the sky gray . . .

From Faial to Pico one can go in a motorized vessel or under sail. The sailing vessel is splendid, but the oil-fired one has its charm. There are big ones that can carry sixty passengers, and there are smaller ones, that can take twelve to fifteen and can withstand strong gales. One such vessel, caught up in a cyclone, once ended up at Terceira, where just one crew member survived, because he stubbornly remained inside, even after the engine had stalled, clutching the wooden planks with the despair of a shipwrecked sailor. One travels inside a cabin, with little square windows, wooden bulkheads on either side: if one looks out, the sea is right there, blue and ever-present; if one wants, one can talk to the other passengers, women from Pico, their shawls pulled down over their head, concealing their brow like

nuns, men with leather sandals and straw hats, on their way
to market, loaded with sacks and baskets, which they stow
under the seats. Pico cannot get by without Faial, where it
buys corn and wheat, and Faial needs Pico, which provides it
with wine, timber, and fruit. But more interesting is the boat,
with a crew of twenty or so men, a master and first mate,
which plies the route between the two islands every day, and
at more or less fixed times, carrying cattle, barrels of wine,
and all manner of cargo loaded onto it. Sailing boats serve
the ports of Madalena, Calhau, Cais do Pico, and Prainha do
Norte. They are large, unwieldy craft, with roughly hewn
wooden benches, lots of cables and pulleys, but they use two
sails and angle through the sea at speed, opening up great
furrows in the waters like a plow.

The worst winds for sailing are the west-southwesterlies,
and the easterlies, of which they say, "An east wind brings no
good," but today it is a northeasterly, fresh but not gusting
too hard, what they call a "general wind." I sit at the stern
and take this all in: the master, who is a boy; the first mate,
an old man of eighty, deeply etched face and as stout as a
beam, who sits next to me and tells me his name, José Faria;
the big, burly, dark-skinned lads of Pico; the women, huddled
in the well of the vessel; the basket weavers and traders from
different Pico parishes, who came to sell their wares and are
returning home. All of them wear a straw hat on their head,
with the brim turned up and tied with a black ribbon, and
sandals on their feet—a thick sole attached by leather straps,
one over the toes and the other round the ankle.

"Come about. Hold your tack," the master, standing at
the helm, recommends to the old man, who is his father and
who is holding the rope. When the weather is bad, or there
is a strong wind, the man with the tack never lets go of it
and the master, by the helm, signals to him from where he is

standing. They do not exchange a word. They communicate by means of gestures.

"Come about!"

They call these two large triangular sails lateens, and they are full of patches like beggars' clothes—the larger one at the bow is the foresail, the smaller one is just called the sail. When the master orders, "Trim the mainsail," he is always referring to the smaller sail.

I approach the old man, whose breath is fresh and whose teeth are as white as a boy's. He has been doing the Pico route for fifty years, always in his shirt sleeves and bare chested, whether in summer or winter. And he is eighty.

"I've had some funny crossings . . . Once, it was Francisco da Ritinha who was in charge, he's the one who lives in the house on the corner. I told him: 'Be careful, see how the tide is running into the wind.' He didn't take any notice, and we were at death's door . . . We toiled away for five hours without even getting halfway across. We had to go back."

"How do you manage to stay as fit as a young boy, sir?"

"I'll tell you how it's done . . . Marry late, get widowed early, don't eat salty or sour things, and stay out of arguments."

The rigging and mast in the keelson are creaking. We are not far from the islets off Madalena, huge red rocks almost next to Pico. From time to time, the bow rises and comes crashing down into the sea, sending out rolls of white surf on either side. A couple of minutes and then we are out of it.

Sailboats link Ribeira, Santo Amaro, and Cais do Pico with São Jorge, Graciosa, and Terceira. Between Flores and Corvo it is more serious—the channel is frightening; not long ago, a sailboat disappeared without trace, crew and all. But business is tempting, and they make the crossing loaded with lime and roof tiles. From Angra to Ponta Delgada, they carry tobacco and general cargo and, from Ponta Delgada to the other islands, wood and Lagoa china. They carry corn, tiles, and clay pots from Santa Maria, vessels like this sailboat I see in front of me, called the Espírito Santo, with a master and seven crew. And from Ponta Delgada, during the season, ships with two lateens, set out loaded with fruit.

My God, how I take everything in! My gaze follows little paths that lead to goodness knows where, and down which a man is walking with his donkey and its load; my eyes fasten on certain places and houses where I would like to live hidden away, not only my life but all the other lives. And my soul reaches out to these boats of all shapes and sizes that arrive and leave . . . Where to? Where to? . . . How would I know where to? To places I have never seen—towards color and light. To hell with the liars who lead us in the ways of deception—and, along with them, attorneys, at the back of their offices surrounded by their useless piles of paper, the clerks in their lairs, the military men with plumes on their head and rusty swords hanging by their side, and the army of clowns that guard our registry offices! . . . Oh! How I wish I were the captain of a boat going from island to island, touching in at ports, a blue bonnet with red edging on my head and my hand on the helm, with my heavy cargo of apricots, ripe apricots bursting with juice that would fill the quay with their fragrance and that I would sell for the time-honored price of one *tostão* for a hundred! . . . What a pleasure it would be to leave as night falls, in full sail, taking advantage of the wind off the land, and under the pulsating stars! Or at the end of the afternoon, the keel cutting a royal highway through the water, gold from ship to horizon. The sea is like honey! . . . By day, the islands loom up out of the channels, unfolding, their capes and promontories taking on sharper focus. If we are in the São Jorge channel, we can see Faial in the distance, a flat-topped mountain that is distinguishable from Pico when we reach mid-channel, while the elongated shape of São Jorge lies behind us, light and dark green, with a cloud clinging to its highest parts. On the other side, Pico emerges from the water all blue, from water where blue mingles with gray, with almost golden undulations. Sometimes the weather changes; the wind turns; gray, foam-crested waves advance from the south: a cloud-colored opaqueness falls over the sea, and, in the distance, dense clouds accumulate over ever bigger waves . . . But I am not afraid; it is in this sailing ship that I sense the presence of my ancestral souls. For me, there is nothing to compare with a few hours on the sea, sails billowing, feeling the waves slapping against the vessel's hull—a feeling of calm and at the same time exaltation, of a boundless, uncomplicated life. The vibrant air fills my lungs; the waves crash on the surface in little eddies of foam that look like flowers. Just as in the oldest, most primitive machines, the first attempts to dominate nature, everything here is deployed with simplicity, devoid of prior experience. We experience the same feeling we have before great pieces of sculpture, the statue's hand and fingers that imbue it with life. We feel the hand and its creator. In primitive mills, in waterwheels for drawing water from rivers, there is a tentative quality, something missing that lends them more humanity than perfect machines: they almost always creak and groan—they suffer like we do. And, for me, their pain, their flaws give them added magic. Here, the masts are gnarled, the sails patched and in pieces, like a beggar's rags. One comes across ropes and cables everywhere. There is no engine to drive it forward—we must rely on the wind: if it is not blowing, then the journey lasts an eternity. We must rely on God: at every turn, we feel we are in his hands. Man has done all that is possible; now He must do the rest.

I look. As the land fades into the distance, the blue begins
to fade. The small waves grow in size and the wind picks up.
There is a sudden gust. There is a sound of metal grating.
Then, it is the timber that groans with pain, shot through by
the same agitation that passed through the air. The whole
vessel feels it from bow to stern, rising in order to crash into
the sea as it froths. The sail flaps and fills, and billows out like
a full belly. Further out to sea, the space is as empty as the sky,
glinting with jewels, and before me, the sheer, dark coast slips
by more rapidly. I feel like grabbing the helm. I have to stop
myself from issuing gruff commands:

"Watch your tack, boys! . . . Come about! Come about
now!"

Sete Cidades and Furnas

In front of me, I see the escarpment with a lonely bell tower, undulations and windmills, a large blue-toned hill in the distance, and a beach that ends with a screen of low hills of about the same size. Half an hour later, I enter the port of Ponta Delgada. It is a small, irregular, and cheerful city, ranged along the seashore, with its green hills in the background: an occasional ungainly, ghostly figure passes down the street, swathed in a wide-hooped cape. In this placid, green landscape, with a sky the texture of blotting paper overhead, my eyes are drawn to that violet hill with the Lagoa at its base . . .

Clean streets, a square, a pretty church, and marvelous gardens—that of Jácome Correia is well maintained and functional, with huge dreamlike trees and, over there, in the background, next to the palace, hedges of tomatoes and rows of potatoes fertilized with potash; the António Borges garden has a little valley of lacy plants, where one plunges into a delicate, green light, a light that suggests putrescence, amid

this family of ferns that spring from a dewy carpet of moss. It
smells of earth and dampness. And the stillness in which these
admirably delicate plants grow, their plumed leaves, whether
tall or minute, perfect miniatures not exceeding the size of
lichens, causes me to lower the tone of my voice. Better: the
green light and the misty silence, pierced by a sole ray of sunlight from above slipping in like a spider's thread and illumi-
nating a single spot of ground, force me to pause in order not
to disturb what seems to me an extraordinary intercourse. I
spend most time in the José do Canto garden, which is of a
dense, magnetic green. Trees that inspire respect, with grot-
tos and caverns in their trunks, scenic trees, full of strength
and width or fragile and transparent as glass—a piece of the
tropics transported by magic to Ponta Delgada, and which, if
I had time, I would start to explore as if it were virgin forest.
With regard to the city's gardens, I am left with an impression of stifling heat, damp warmth, deep shadow, a religious
silence, and a bird singing . . . Such solitude with abandoned
trees (I always walk on tiptoe inside large gardens, because
there is always present some enchanted spirit in communication with me) has remained rooted in me forever after.
Houses are always the same, men the same everywhere you
go. But this is not the case with gardens. Neither the gardens
nor the convent of Esperança, whose tall, dense tower I cannot forget, built for eternity, and the grated windows that fill
us with fear. Stronger, heavier than a prison, it weighs on our
chest and deprives us of air. This, perhaps, was the impression left on Antero,[19] for it was here, sitting on a bench under
its walls, that, after looking everywhere for a way out, he
released himself from life.

---

[19] Antero de Quental (1842–91) was a philosopher and poet from the
Azores. He committed suicide in his native city of Ponta Delgada (translator's note).

But there are two marvelous things on this island: Furnas and Sete Cidades. It frightens me almost, today, to speak of a landscape that now seems more unreal than ever . . .

August 1

I pass through Feteiras, Ribeira da Candelária, Lomba da Cruz, and set off towards Cumieira, now among crevices as I ascend the side of the hill, now along bluffs that look out over farmland down below extending as far as the sea—land that is divided, gashed, scarred by mudslides. Over the pallid sea, which stands in contrast to the dark velvet of the land, float delicate shreds of cloud—a sign of calm.

"Going up is the difficult part," the man accompanying me says. "Even a lame goat can make the journey down . . ."

Just another few steps and we arrive at the cliff from where one suddenly glimpses Sete Cidades hidden away among the hills. It is the highest point of Cumieira: I have the lakes at my feet and, if I turn round, the wide vista that takes in a major part of the island, sea, sky, and coastline, bathed in light and immateriality.

The sea, in all its amplitude, is a flat expanse at an acute angle with the flat green of the land—and it looks as if it is about to crash over it. In front of me, an abyss opens up that casts us out of life, to unexpected regions of the dream world. Convulsion, brute force, and fire raised great volcanic cliffs up into the sky, leaving at the bottom of this chaos one or two gentle areas of grassland and two lakes, one completely green, the other completely blue, separated by a narrow isthmus, quiet, slumbering, and brooding. All the forces unleashed resulted in this: a little blue, a little green, a mellow idyll . . . Steeply hewn cliffs, covered with trees tumbling their entire length, ending at the water's edge or in little flat fields of corn, which the island light envelops in a pure, motionless frigidity . . .

A gasp of astonishment, a new feeling, a vague feeling of surprise . . . For the first time in my life, I do not know how to describe what I see and feel. I am acquainted with the voluptuous lakes of Italy, and the sleeping lochs of Scotland. The lake of Sete Cidades resembles none that I have seen. Does that still water exist, or have I imagined it? That great primordial hollow dusted with purple, with that captive serenity at its base? This strange beauty that will not let go of us and contemplates us at the same time that we contemplate it?

The character of the landscape is subtle and concealed. Although we can see the belfry and the tiny houses on the floor of the huge crater, we doubt our vision and even reach the point of assuming that a magician has waved his wand to stop time, and the scene has remained preserved in its enchantment among harsh, boundless hills, which are its prison guards. Time passes, men pass; only down there is everything suspended, fixed in its original state. In this magical solitude, one cannot hear a bird sing, the water does not move, the flowers do not move. Everything can be seen in the vast width of the crater, open to the sky and bathed in a petrified silence. So little hue! This is a picture made of emotion; a picture in which green is not quite green, in which blue is mist, and the purple dust hanging in the air a mere puff, the unadulterated breath of the landscape as it gasps. Three delicate strips coordinate the enchantment, as if it were possible to paint a masterpiece only with feeling and without any colors. I notice that there are in fact some tracks lost among the hills which lead down to the crater's floor. But I dare not follow them! I am afraid that if I get too near this vision it will vanish into thin air!

I start to notice details: on one side, the lava opened up furrows, which are etched all the way down the slope. Shadows of clouds hover over the waters and turn into green haze on one lake and blue haze on the other, at the same time as the green of the escarpments gradually melts into the waters. With each passing minute, the light transforms the thick ramparts, the hardy spurs sheltered and hidden in their midst with an air of drama—and, at the same time, they see themselves reproduced in the tranquil waters—those two crystalline jewels, one of each color, both paralyzed with bewilderment. One moment, everything becomes frozen still, remote and absent, seen through glass, and then the purple takes possession of the green, the great shadows of the valley grow darker, and the landscape floats in a thin blue mist like a ghost as it passes into another life—a soul ascending and disappearing into the air. I stretch out my hands . . .

I have already seen this before, and it was not in the light of a flame, where I usually glimpse the other world. One winter's day, my window was covered in frost, delicate curlicues, spider's webs spun by the night's chaste hands, and, as morning broke in all its purity, the pale sun warmed it and turned it gold. It was a fragile, useless piece of nothingness that filled me with awe and dreaminess; it was the most beautiful of landscapes and jewels, reflected on the windowpane, only to disappear from the universe in a moment. I suspect that Sete Cidades is also the soul of a landscape. The great landscapes that die must go and meet somewhere . . . God placed it here, devoted and chaste, at the bottom of this huge crater, amid fire and chaos; He surrounded it with solitude and mountains; He placed the sea around it all so as to defend it. But one gets the impression it feels a yearning and seeks to break the spell: shrouded in its thin mist, it dreams, floats, and takes on a vaguely sad air: it aspires to be still more otherworldly—it will flicker and disappear into the ether . . .

This is why I feel there is something eerie about it. It belongs to a life of the spirit—it is the ghost of a landscape. The hues are fragile and shot through with feeling; life is static and motionless. The enchanted princess of the legend

I hear so much about must dwell there, hidden beneath the
waters, emerging on nights pregnant with moonlight to take
possession of her realm . . .

I only regain a sense of reality as I return, halfway back, at
Areal, next to a source of flowing fresh water, amid monkey
puzzles and Japanese cedars, plane trees and huge ferns. It is
a delicious, icy filament of water, born from a stone hidden
among the moss.

August 4

The island of São Miguel is all more or less mountainous,
with some high peaks. The eastern and western parts of the
island contain the highest: Pico da Vara is 1,105 meters and
949 at Lagoa do Fogo; 847 meters at Pico das Éguas, etc. The
central region in between, from Ponta Delgada to Ribeira
Grande, is scattered with volcanic cones, which are much
lower in height. From Povoação to the northeast, the land is
all irregular, with deep valleys, magnificent ravines, and sudden unforeseen features that are reminiscent of a small-scale
Switzerland lost in mid-ocean. But in general, one could say
that the lowest part is along the coast, the hills being distributed along the central regions of the island.

Good use is made of the land; even the *biscoitos*—the
remains of lava fields—produce timber. Pineapples are cultivated in the deeper, more sheltered terrain; tea on the higher,
more humid parts; and corn in all the valleys.

I travel by car along the roads in order to get an idea of
some of the features of country life. People seem to live a
carefree existence. In the humble churches and single-story
houses, the floor is covered in pine needles for the women
to sit on. We enter one of these houses and are immediately
captivated: it smells of pine, sun, and the hills, and everything
is spotlessly clean. Outside are the granaries built on four

whitewashed legs, the *cafuão,* a thatched shelter where the corn is laid to dry and which is used for storage and sometimes even as a room, or covered with a tarpaulin, speckled with yellow, corresponding to the number of ears of grain that can fit in one's hand, a familiar, rustic scene in small-scale farming, blessed by God, and where everything has been put in its appropriate place since time immemorial. One gets the impression that women lead happy lives: in the north, a woman works alongside the man in tobacco cultivation, collecting and packing the leaves; in Bretanha, women are well known as farmers; in the south, she normally involves herself in domestic tasks—spinning wool and flax. These days, it is rare to find a farmer wearing a cape with a hood over his head and brow, and a flap draped over his shoulders. One may still come across such trappings in Arrifes, where older ways of life persist.

The countryside is full of birds where the little species seem to live happily—the lined seedeater or Our Lady's hen, which on Terceira is called a *ferifolha,* or warbler, and which has a star on its head to distinguish it, the smallest bird on São Miguel; the courageous wagtail, which follows the buzzard and pecks it under its wing; the saffron finch, the blackbird, and the gray tanager. Only one malevolent creature sticks its narrow neck out of cracks in old walls and watches them— the stoat, or *comadrinha,* as some people here call it.

This blessed land produces everything; its richest soil produces coffee, peanuts, pineapple, tea, and everywhere, there are the fruits grown on the mainland. I was in a hurry to see the tea and pineapple crops, of which I was unaware, and I was surprised by the sight of those plantations of squat bushes laid out in ordered lines across the hills. Here and there, a Moluccan albizia provides the shade that this type of camellia requires. In the midst of the bushes, groups of young girls pick the youngest leaves, dropping them in a basket carried over their arm. The tea plant, constantly sacrificing itself in this way from May to September, obstinately alive and sprouting anew, puts out more shoots and leaves, which are then picked. I drank the best tea in the Azores, light and aromatic, at Gorriana, the country house of Mr. Jaime Hintze, all single storied and painted with yellow limewash, amid the happy bustle of rustic life, in a home blessed by his wife's kindness. I went to see the cultivation of pineapples at Fajã de Baixo, in the large greenhouses belonging to that illustrious Azorean lady, Dona Alice Moderno. This delicious fruit, with leaves like zinc, is harvested still green for transport, but if you wait for it to ripen in the greenhouse, its perfume will make your mouth water. With persistent heat and constant humidity, producing vapor as it is on the point of flowering, you will obtain a huge, delicious strawberry from the shriveled black stump of its root. I have little interest in the vast, low greenhouses, where they grow in orderly ranks, in virgin soil where thousands of plants need to be uprooted with such regularity. What I would like is to wander through the tropical forest on a hot day until exhausted, and then come upon a family of ripe pineapples . . .

The features of the land I am traveling through vary continually before my eyes. Now there are fields of corn and beets, divided by robust reed hedges—always the same fields, always the same reeds in cultivated lowlands (such as along the road from Ponta Delgada to Mosteiro); now there are low hills, pinewoods, and ridges, followed by the different vistas of the coast.

On the way to Furnas, alongside rows of elm trees or beneath the branches of plane trees forming colorful, transparent canopies with golden curtains, I come across carts carrying virgin soil for the greenhouses. The little houses painted with yellow limewash, at first all clustered together, become sparser the further away we get. All we see as we proceed, there in the background, is a line of hillocks resembling blisters. On every estate we pass, we see the white glass of greenhouses. Pineapple is king. Occasionally, we pass a house with a wide entrance gate, a noble courtyard, and eighteenth-century windows. The road climbs and the road descends, and the vegetation is ever thicker and more unrestrained. By now, there is a glimmering whiteness in the distance—Ribeira Grande. The vista becomes wider, but clouds begin to pad the sky and the smell of dampness pervades my nostrils. All this bountiful, purified air begins to burn. The heat makes one languid. One more stretch of road sloping upwards, and I see before me the fertile plain of Ribeira Grande, a wide tableau of varying tones, from the golden yellow of the wheat to the dark green of the corn. In the background, across the whole width of the sky, there is the static outline of a cloud, stretched out like an awning, allowing a few rays of sunlight to illuminate the ocean, while the countryside remains swathed in a whitened, magnetic clarity right up to the range of gray hills. In the other direction, everything fuses with the agglomeration of clouds on the horizon. I have already seen this wide, even, bounteous landscape, with the same light and the same soil enriched by water and humus, elsewhere in some place I cannot recall, all bathed in a mist that muffles sound and dissipates color . . . It is green, powerful, sweeping, and at the same time seems to exude elation, as if the breeze were rippling its nerves over the crops. The vast, tense plain quivers under a shadow that bears no weight and which gently bends the stalks of rye and wheat . . . But the automobile speeds onwards and another sharp bend reveals the sea, glimpsed between bluish pine-woods descending to Santa Iria. A few more kilometers and the view changes once again at Ladeira Velha, with a coast-line that is green and clear-cut or else diluted in the haze, a wide panorama of shadows, watery tints, mists streaked with folds of green, indistinct until the vaporous purple, until the dark green down by the seashore. A series of capes, inlets, and rocks can be just made out under the gray sky shot through with shafts of light, padded with mist, through which one can sense the sun pulsating. One can see the flat, purple sea, and a hillside covered with pines next to it. One can see the José do Canto building in Porto Formoso, from where whaleboats set out. São Brás: I ask the driver to stop in order to survey the land and the sky, as if we were on the mountain top where Satan tempted Jesus.

Above all, we are faced with a tone here, a tone I wish to make a specific note of at this point, because I have never seen its like anywhere else: a gray that is infinitely graded, the gray of these days when the sun mingles with mist, and which only belongs to the Azores, where the land takes on all the nuances of gray, from purplish-gray to leaden gray, with lighter shades of gray further away. It is a gray composed of mist and sunlight that hovers over the wide, humid landscape. A gray nearby that clings to the trees and constantly varies in tone, from a pearly color to one that contains a trace of gold, depending on the distances, the breeze, the clouds passing over and receding, transforming the picture all the time and turning the plain into a large, moving scene in which new decorative motifs are forever appearing.

It is not the same as other places. It is richer. On this vast, cultivated plain, gray acquires another life, other tones, and greater variety. Sometimes it tumbles into filaments of light. It is almost nothing; it is the slightest puff that fades and then increases and pours out over the whole countryside, shelter-ing it, enriching it. I have never seen it so mobile and fused with the surroundings as here, so bursting with effects and assimilating colors to the point of making them somewhat remote, while at the same time infusing them with life. Fragile and vague, dreamlike. There is a sadness, of course, but it possesses the strange magic of springtime that cannot quite burst into life.

It is a light that caresses me, a range of grays that run into each other and fade, catch just a little light and become absorbed and quiet, or else they create new life and reignite a whole array of tones that would make a painter despair, for the landscape in this extraordinary light gains shadows, a diversity and a freshness that paintbrushes are unable to reproduce . . . It is the last time I shall see it, and I take my leave for good. I have to say that I am getting a little tired and yearn for another light . . . I am starting to miss the old sunbaked wall in my garden, where buttercups grow, along with yellow and pink lichens, and even the stones ripen like grapes! . . .

August 6

I cross the plateau, or *Achada,* of Furnas, a desolate region, until I reach the twisted spine of the Trigo mountain range. I descend the Pedras do Galego and between breathtaking bluffs, the splendid valley of Furnas opens out before me. It is a basin surrounded by hills—Pico do Bode, Lagoa Seca, Pico de Ferro, and Pico do Cavaleiro. At the bottom of the crater, little houses hidden amongst the greenery and a stark contrast between the slate-colored bluffs and one or two little fields of young corn, which one feels like caressing with one's hand; between the crater's basin full of trees and water, and the volcano funneled and reduced to a few plumes of vapor that seep out of round protective walls, and the great mountain ranges that it spewed out and produced. Now, it is only there to make us feel slightly uneasy—to give us greater sensuous pleasure . . . Under the crust upon which we tread, and which must only be a few meters thick, the inferno survives, of course: all one would need to do is to dig the soil with the end of a walking cane to open up a flue.

This constant heat and humidity explains the sudden profusion of abundant greenery. Trees grow before our eyes. What takes centuries to develop elsewhere, is achieved over a few years here—but what lasts for centuries elsewhere is over in an instant here, tired of putting down roots, throwing limbs up into the air, or bursting out in foliage and flowers. All trees will take from shoots. Fruit trees grow, produce layers of fruit, and then soon finish. Heat and humidity. The soil warmed by the sun, sheltered by the mountains, and watered by streams of hot, subterranean water that flow into the lake produces yams with huge leaves of a green that is almost black, and corn the height of two men. I pass along a grove: the leafy plants are the size of trees; water falls, it turns the waterwheel, irrigates the fields, and soaks the roots of the araucarias, the banana trees, the bamboos, as thick as tree trunks. Is this some corner of a tropical forest? No, it is a little garden. Such excesses must be paid for in some way. Such exuberance, when it is as impetuous as this, is always two steps away from destruction. Life's rhythms have become accelerated. And perhaps this is why I am haunted by the idea of death amidst all this extraordinary vegetation. I begin to ponder on the fact that right under my feet, the volcano continues to simmer away in goodness knows what sort of mixture, casting out excess vapor through the crater, occasionally in a fearsome cloud of smoke. There are occasions when this inferno is pacified. I peer at the water boiling away in the saucepans which go by the names of the Murada crater, the crater of Pero Botelho, and the Esguicho crater, which emits a spray, and several more besides. There are four larger ones and one or two holes that contain bubbling gases or spit out jets of mud. One of these, the Polme crater, emits a grayish powder from somewhere below, with the mournful noise of someone in their death throes. But everywhere, the water boils profusely. The atmosphere is impregnated with carbon dioxide and sulfur. It smells. Cold waters mix with hot, on the surface or below ground, rising to the surface through wells or gurgling from sources of all types and good for all manner of illnesses—ferrous or acidic, icy or boiling, brackish and radioactive—for the liver, for the eyes, the stomach, for rheumatism, in quantities and blends that may even be harmful . . .

Such is the origin of all this abundance of greenery. The blue cedar is indigenous, the faya is indigenous, as is the ailanthus and a few more . . . All the other trees are imported, and grow as profusely here as they would at home, if not more so. There is heat, some magnetism in the atmosphere I cannot describe, a winter when rain falls continuously, washing topsoil down from the mountains and mixing it with the chemical elements that fertilize the soil, and all this explains why, inside this magnificent circus, plant life is so prodigious. There are one or two marvelous parks, some little whitewashed houses, two or three with a gentlemanly air—and a false tranquility, the air of one who does this ostentatiously in order to delude us and leave us dizzy—possibly to catch us unawares . . . But I am calm and collected, and I am certainly not going to sleep on top of a volcano . . . And I would not spend much time next to these huge, mute creatures, these hulks that fill me with apprehension. I always remember, and I can see it right in front of me, that forest of Daudet's which ends up devouring a town. There are giants here, before which one pauses, and which drag us towards the unknown. I start communicating with them, and cannot understand them. Naturally, I am not afraid of a tree to whose company I have become accustomed. Nor am I frightened of trees in a general sense. But when they are entirely unknown, when they take on these proportions, when they form dense, entangled forests, when they start whispering to each other at night—then my only desire is to escape. Even the shapes of the plants in the gardens here are not of this world. Only a short time ago, I came across one plant full of red flowers, already familiar to me from some other mysterious life . . . I find myself walking along paths that make me languid and brooding, and only some days after having visited Furnas do I dare to enter parks with the utmost stealth—the parks of António Borges, Albano da Ponte, Marquês da Praia, Beatriz do Canto, and José do Canto.

Green, a still, static green that is reflected in the foul-smelling waters of the lakes, in more somber greens—in the pustular, alluvial water—causing a shiver that tears them away from their ordered immobility. There are gigantic elms, oak trees extending their muscular arms everywhere, weeping willows leaning over and dipping their nervous threads in the quietude of the lake, rows of ferns flaunting their lacy tails in the air. A brook flows through the middle of the park, rupturing it with voices and murmurs. I strike out among the trunks, listening to the crunch of the sand under my feet; I pause in front of the rust-colored pond; I follow the lane which opens out into an avenue of palms, with flowers halfway up their trunks in the shape of a candelabra, and I rest in the dark shadows, where the sun cannot penetrate, listening to the birds singing . . . Before me, there is another serpentine lake with the green threads of weed spread out on the surface of the water like hair. In this water that reflects the blue of the hydrangeas, the lines of the ferns in great detail, the trunks erect like pillars, the effects of the light are extraordinary. It imbibes all the tones, reproduces all the colors . . . The putrefying elements create a blue film, through which there is a glimmer of jewels; the leaves are mirrored one by one in the glassy film; the sky is represented in the middle by a motionless shard, and down below the frog-green decomposes to the point of smelling. The fleeting dragonfly glistens and disappears, and at the end of a path covered by layer upon layer of leaves, the punishing sunlight gleams through the darkness as if we were at the bottom of a well. I cross the stone bridge, next to huge fallen trees. Banks of bracken and an effusion of tree ferns burst from the sloping verge.

I am on my way to see Povoação, and the scenes that follow are all different. The road climbs in twists and curves amidst trees with their roots embedded in the base of the Trigo range of hills. Huge plane trees, eucalyptuses, acacias. A lush valley on one side and, in front, a hill and a steep bluff. All this has the air of a forest where one very occasionally comes across a sawmill filling the whole road with a resinous smell. And, as the car progresses, the deep gullies and the woods spin in a whirl, the valleys change, the verdant hills move, pass by me, and disappear. I do not even have time to admire the fresh clusters of hydrangeas that cover the roadside verges, or that narrow aperture that opens out onto the valley floor. But I manage to focus on a group of men in the process of felling a tree, a woman passing by with a bundle of firewood for the oven, the picturesque movement of the road . . . Cliff faces open out and narrow in the same instant. We climb ever higher . . . Suddenly, through a crag, I catch a glimpse of the blue sea between the green escarpments. Then the road starts to descend and cultivated land reappears, fields of corn, the golden threshing floors with the straw stripped of its grain. It is at this point on the route that we suddenly catch our first sight of Povoação—a series of parallel rolling hillocks down below, each one with its row of little white houses, Lomba

do Carro, Lomba do Botão, Lomba do Pomar, Alcaide, etc.,
in equal lines, as if drawn with a ruler, green and cultivated.
Behind, the sierra, with the Pico da Vara and Lavaçal. On one
side, the sea invades the land through a sharp, angular cut
in the coastline. What completes the beauty of this sweeping panorama of toil and of light is the way the mountains
and the ocean complement each other. We breathe in all this
vastness with joy: our lungs are replenished when we leave
the valleys, where the cliffs crush us. From high up, one can
see the cattle, the threshing floors, the bustle of people at
work, the familiar details of rural life, all on a small scale, in
miniature, as in those primitive Flemish paintings. A family
reposes by its front door; further away, a farmer yokes his
oxen to the cart . . . The impression gained is one of peace
and abundance. Everything looks effortless, the crops grown
in neat and orderly fields as far as the hillsides and the vigorous, bountiful plantations of corn that one sees growing
everywhere. Povoação is the island's granary.

I return to Furnas in order to visit the José do Canto park. A
few kilometers along a little road that skirts the gardens and
we come in sight of the large lake at Furnas, green among
green pines that grow right down to the water's edge from
on high. In the background, the Gothic chapel and the house
that belonged to José do Canto; behind it, the vast woodland,
where everything grows wild, in accordance with his final
wishes. The chapel does not interest me. I have never been
interested in funeral monuments. On the contrary, lack of
humility and understanding of nature and of life have always
been a source of irritation to me. It is enough for the dead
to issue the orders that are already issued to the living. To
impose themselves upon us until the end of time, that seems

a little too much to me . . . All the better that the park overwhelms everything—the park that was this man's dream, and
who stipulated that it should remain untouched until the third
generation had passed. Nothing is pruned. Until recently, not
even the wood that fell from the trees was collected from the
ground. And this, I can understand. What a dream to take
to one's tomb! I would feel the spring right next to me. The
autumn I would feel it even when turned to dust. And the
struggle of the forest, turning itself over, growing, advancing, unable to bear the weight of its branches. Don't touch it!
All I would ever want is to remain ever closer to its roots . . .

It is the great mass of waving trees that is all important
here, trees clutching each other desperately, the enclosed
darkness and single beam of light that comes from above,
alighting on the soil with its golden stain. A cavern. A dark
corridor and at the end a faded golden light. One enters a
great subterranean cave where light barely filters through the
thick mesh of canopies. Tropical trees, trees from all climates
and countries, the *ficus, metrosidus,* camellia, and varieties
of palm trees live in a dim half-light. The azaleas are enormous, and there are parts of the park which are impossible
to untangle, as if they were virgin forest. Lianas intertwine
in the opaque, mysterious depths. There is a smell of jungle
humidity and man perhaps feels more like those green, placid
life forms that grow in accordance with the benign laws of
nature, accepting life without contesting it. It is the example
they give me and that I cannot accept . . . I set off, full of emotion, into a fern-covered valley, down a verdant, putrid, mysterious little glade . . . There are ferns of all different shapes
and varieties. I walk around and climb the slope in order to
look down on their delicate leaves from a higher position.
They are feminine plants, full of sensitivity and restlessness.
From above, the abundance of greenery and its splendid
vestments cannot be fully appreciated when viewed in the

light filtered through the layers of foliage, the dark green, the luminous green, the green shot through with sunlight, the green that trembles. But the green is overbearing. Only the green fills the world, as if the world belonged to vegetation. The sensation one gets is one of fatigue, and it even draws our breath away. Such grandeur is an imposition. A tree takes on exaggerated importance. It is as if the kingdom of this world and the other belonged to it. I love trees—but here, they expect me to adore them in perpetuity. Let us work together, if you want. Give me some shade, exchange views with me, but please let me glimpse the architecture of the world. I occasionally feel like slashing open the vegetation with an axe in order to see the sky. This is not a piece of orderly parkland—it is a jungle. All of a sudden, I find myself lost in a forest next to fallen trees, hundreds of miles from the world, or in a sun-filled clearing with tiny groves of fruit trees waving their branches this way and that. The entire forest floor is covered with apples and limes. It is such a waste. All around, there is the smell of fruit, which is a consolation.

Picture the drizzly season and springtime in these parks. Imagine the bare trees and the azaleas and rhododendrons below full of flowers. One can sense the vitality, hear the leaves sprouting, the eruption of colors and the hum rising into the light from deep underground. But the true spring here is autumn, when each tree resembles a gigantic flower and Furnas takes on the tones of another ethereal world. I love the fading autumns, the fine rain, when the leaves drop from the trees one by one. It is a gentle end to life, full of yearning that only passes slowly . . . These autumns are different—they are apotheoses, wonderment; another source of energy that does not accept death and clings desperately to life. There is passion in this never-ending agony. Just as life was prodigious in its fecundity, in their final days, all the trees complain, all the trees protest . . . Some of these giants

rise into the air all red, and the plane trees in torches of melting gold. There are some that stand out, bloodied against
the amorphous backdrop; there are those that are gradually stripped of their leaves, rust-colored, dying, screaming
while they decompose. One can see extraordinary bronze
hues and gold—rose—crimson—while others remain almost
green in their death throes. There are paler colors—yellows,
at the same time tinged with green and gold, incredible
corrosive, acidic gradations. And along with all this, a subdued melancholy and the smell of a cemetery in fermenta-
tion. The ground is a sumptuous mat which one treads on
with apprehension. This astounding autumn is perhaps the
most beautiful season at Furnas, deceptive as it deludes the
senses, ecstatic and at the same time magical. It is a mineral
illness. Prior to death, all of the trees, like all women, resist,
undaunted, and cake their skin, ready for the sepulcher, with
salts of copper, opulent, varied salts—unable to conceal the
terrible hour of despair and old age.

I enjoy watching it get dark among these green stains,
where one can still just make out one or two tiny shreds of
light between the leaves. I gaze at the hills that are ever darker
and more fearsome. I look up at the crests of the hills and
they are like a colander through which the last rays of light
are filtered, while down below, the shadow settles down for
the night. One starts to hear the water babble more loudly.
As the mountains grew, the village became smaller, until it
disappeared. The craters vomit plumes of vapor. In the pitch
darkness in which the massive sweep of background vegetation appears twice as imposing in terms of size and degree
of blackness, ever darker and more indistinct, only one or
two stars manage to glimmer through the leaves and reach
us. Only one thing fills the world and speaks ever louder: the
noise of the waters, the voice of the sources gushing forth,
of tinkling little fountains and their trickling water, all the

voices in unison, but which I can distinguish one by one, from the voice of the brook breaking over pebbles, to the water cascading over the weir, to its fervent bubbling, all of which joins in a melody that cools and enchants the solitary night of Furnas.

The Azorean Atlantic

This ocean has a solemn, brooding appearance. We leave in the morning when the sea is flat, and we return home in the afternoon, with the sea dark and seething. When we least expect it, the wind blows up and, from mid-August onwards, we may catch a storm. The crossing from Faial to Corvo is dangerous and from Corvo to Flores is almost always menacing. Sometimes small vessels such as sailboats and schooners set out and disappear without a trace. The channel between Pico and São Jorge is deeper and, for this reason, calmer. Round here, there are craters concealed beneath the waters, and lava occasionally comes to the surface, even forming a whole island that then soon disappears. To the nature of these waters, subject to sudden fits of temper, we could add that of the land, which trembles almost every day (Faial), causing hearts to miss a beat, that of the otherworldliness produced by the volcanic coasts, by the hesitant light that stops, transforms itself, revealing a high peak, dramatic cliffs, and lands that do not exist and are a magical effect of the clarity itself that is shrouded in mist. Grace, elegance, rose tints infuse the gray sea, which, for that very reason, seems still wider: clouds waft up out of craters like vapor; sunbeams of bib- lical proportions pass through the massed cumuli; the light is damp, the light is filtered through ragged shreds of cloud, through mists that are created quite suddenly, producing sin- gular effects . . . But our spirit is always haunted by doubt . . . Sometimes, when the sea is calm and the sky clear, there in that little stretch of water between the islets of Madalena and Pico, a wave begins to grow for no apparent reason. The nearby channel is as smooth as a mirror. But watch out . . . Blue sky and a flat sea—and an often distant storm, will have repercussions on that particular point of the island, without our knowing why. The wind blows up around a headland when one least expects it, and buffets the sails, catching the little craft and hurling it—this has already happened—as far as the coast of the Algarve.

Six months of winter, six months of bad weather, say the mariners of this mysterious ocean that may well conceal Atlantis. In the Azores, spring does not exist because of the icebergs that often pass not very far from Flores. At the same time, the Gulf Stream warms and modifies the temperature, exercising considerable influence over the atmosphere and the waters: I have even dipped my hand in the sea and found it as tepid as blood. Here, there is only one splendid season— June, July, and August. During the other months, the hills are almost always wrapped in their hoods of mist. Pico's hood, which is an exquisitely made calotte of white clouds, and which it occasionally wears on its head, is an infallible barometer—rain in summer or bad weather in winter. And if the cloud at Prainha stretches to the south of the moun- tain, with the hood up above, then a storm is sure to be on the way. Here and there, the coasts have been sliced verti- cally as if by some fantastic axe. Whoever gazes upon them dreams of the huge convulsions that gave rise to the cavities, shadows, darkness, and the ramparts three or four hundred meters high—trachyte and basalt lava, travertine, pumice, scoria. The scorched rock shows us that this place was in the thick of the conflagration.

The Azorean Atlantic, according to Reclus, reaches a depth of 4,000 meters. From Pico to São Jorge, a distance of seventeen kilometers, probes have produced readings of 1,300 meters. When the sea here goes wild, huge, mountainous waves smash against the massive cliffs, echo in the caves, and crash with a terrifying boom. On Corvo, they even reach the village and the cemetery, which are tens of meters above water level, and awaken the dead. The little island shakes, knocked to its very foundations. On the higher ground, distraught men watch ships sink in the foam, unable to go to their aid. Only three years ago, two steamships disappeared into the abyss, vainly asking for help: the telegraph station without wires was not working—and is still not working.

"A more or less circular hurricane, "according to the Prince of Monaco observatory, "formed in the new hemisphere, moves up the Atlantic Ocean in the region of the equator, progresses northeast, sweeping over or skirting the Antilles and the southern United States, veers northeast, breaking in the area separating Newfoundland and England." The great cyclones in effect come from America, but, in the Azores, which lie in the center of the curved trajectory followed by the atmospheric disturbances born in the Atlantic, huge storms are generated, according to Mascart, which travel at speeds that vary from five to twenty-two miles an hour.

The winds spin out of control, always moving from right to left around a central axis, the only point where there is no wind but where huge waves, coming from all directions, collide with each other, billowing up into the sky. The boat cuts along the bottom of the vitreous ravine deep between mountains, or else it turns its prow into the thundering crash of surf.

This monstrous thing reveals it has a life of its own, an intelligence, a cunning as if the spirit of evil dwells within it. Huge and deranged, it doggedly pursues the boat amidst clamor and yelling, tossing dark, ragged crests at it from every side. From time to time, there is a shout, a scream from a cacophonous living creature, or a crash that shakes the entire ship. The men stare in fascination at the immense sinister ogre, the living, dark monster, and they wait. They wait for life or death. They wait for it at the very second when it occurs; they wait for it during a pause in the cataclysm—and then, once again, the hurricane twists around those sorry timbers and unleashes all the furies within it, casting them all together and, with an intense roar, tearing itself to pieces in rage at the same time, while waves hurl themselves forward, pounding endlessly. Anguish, terror—and the monster still all around them, all around, trying to drag them towards a point that is the abyss. The only way of escape is at an angle—escape or die, while the roar of the waves, which rise into the air in order to come crashing down in boiling spume, gets greater and threatens to send that old bucket to the bottom for daring to fight and win. There are spasms of impotent rage as it prepares another formidable assault.

Sometimes the cataclysm assumes an extraordinary grandeur; other times, a dull terror hangs suspended in the sky. The sails are unable to resist and are torn to shreds, and everything in the world seems to be coming to an end. The night is an inferno, the night is tragic. By now, the sky is in torment, an unmoving copper dome, and the waves are growing even bigger and more menacing. It is night. A night full of phosphorescent mountains, from where screamed curses at the ship emerge, along with jets of spume covering it with spittle. As no two storms are alike—each hurricane has its own personality—other times the sailors fancy they can make out, moving towards the horizon as if swept along in a circular lava flow, mouths agape and showing their teeth, or else, in the mineral light and in the approaching swirling eddies that threaten to suck them down, tragic figures, their arms outstretched, trying to clutch at the men lashed to the masts. They are perhaps cetaceous creatures attracted from the deep; or perhaps they are shipwrecked mariners appealing to the living . . .

So what are the sailors thinking at that moment? What are they thinking!? They obey, if they possibly can, their orders, or they look aghast at the pitch-blackness and total chaos unleashed; they look at it as if they were gazing at death, lashed to the masts, without an idea in their head in the face of this cataclysm that swirls and screams. I cannot describe what is happening. It is many things at the same time—but it is mainly the voice, the multiple echoes lodged in my ears, and which reach a point when they are no longer heard. It is a feeling of being less than nothing inside this compactly rolled monster, this living monster that starts screaming in pain in the middle of the ocean and follows its path tearing itself to pieces as it progresses. And there is little else. Incoherence . . . I spent two days clutching a plank, soaking wet from head to foot, unable to take my eyes off that vision of hell. There are those whose gestures are mechanical; there are those who lose any notion of their existence and neither think nor see: all they can do is hear the deep voice, the voice that comes from the densest of depths, the voice of the wind and of the onrush of the mass of dark water that never falls silent. On and on! Not like a succession of clamors—but only one clamor echoing across the Atlantic and the world. The waters sweep the ship. Is there still anyone managing to hold the helm—firm, and imposing his will upon the surrounding chaos? . . . I could make out the shapes of darkness in front of me, but, apart from this, all I could see were scraps flying past, uproar, disconnected things advancing and retreating, darker densities running into each other, vast waves upon waves ejected by rage, hurling themselves forward and mingling in bluish excretions, their crests flashing with light . . . And nothing else, any notion of day or night lost in that hellish world. There are those, too, although this is hard to explain, who sleep on their feet, sleepwalkers, who sleep with their eyes open, glassy and motionless as if they were already dead. All I retained was the sensation of darkness that seemed to be suffering as much as I was, and which burst into screams of affliction from within the dense gloom, spitting pain and darkness at us—and all the time spinning fiendishly, soaking us, already transmuted and bodiless, ready for never-ending universal movement—swirling forever, swirling for all eternity . . . I was never able to reproduce this in ordered words. I felt myself another man in another universe, even going so far as to lose my fear of death in order to concentrate on my vision of that new world—always turning in clamorous uproar, in a spiral that reaches the heavens and the depths of the abyss, forever clamoring against the suffering of mute things, that never uttered a complaint, and at last found a voice to scream . . . And what saves us is clamor, and the monster having a voice, always shouting and eternally bellowing. Imagine the silent whirlpool spinning, vast and black, intangible as a ghost!

This thing obstinately pursues its howling path across the sea, vainly in search of a thought and a soul. At the same time, as it advances almost slowly, it spins on itself madly, at extraordinary speeds, its chimney, which can have a diameter of hundreds of kilometers, sucking up wind and waves and tossing them up into the sky. Of what chance circumstance is this the product? What atmospheric currents? It is the product, according to Rovel—and I believe him—of radiation from the stars over the earth, of a malevolent spirit following trajectories that are possible to sketch out in advance in minute detail, bewailing its pain as it crosses the sea and falling to earth with tremendous destructive force.

What is down there, in the greatest depths of this strange sea—the sea of hurricanes, which generates ocean currents and maybe the *houle,* or swell, a mysterious wave of huge proportions that grows as it advances until it suddenly crashes one peaceful sunny day onto the coast of Morocco? "If we give credit to geology, it is incontestable that at this point in the Atlantic, three million centuries before the appearance of historical man, there was a vast continent forming a land bridge between Europe and North America, between Africa and South America, which disappeared under the waters of the Atlantic." Atlantis must have included part of the Antilles, the Sargasso Sea, the archipelagos of Madeira, the Azores, and Cape Verde. According to the theories of the learned naturalist, Louis Germain, based on fossilized and live fauna, these lands, along with the Canaries, formed part of Plato's Atlantis. It was from there that the civilization originated, which went on to colonize the islands of the Atlantic and part of America, namely Mexico. Frightful cataclysmic events, formidable volcanic eruptions, great earthquakes, caused the sea to rise and swallow up everything, which then disappeared under the waters—leaving one or two isolated peaks here and there.

What is for sure nowadays is rather than the presence of a dead civilization under the sea, there is a living marvel. We know this from the studies led by Edmond Perrier, by the Prince of Monaco observatory, and by its collaborators, Richard and Joubin, "which reveal the existence of living creatures lighting up the darkness of the deep with their wondrous photogenic apparatuses. At a depth of four or five thousand meters, one can find real animal forests—anemones, umbellules, jellyfish, which, in response to various stimuli, emit violet, blue, red-orange flashes." A jellyfish, on the deck of a ship, flashed such a bright light that it could be identified six meters away. Luminous starfish, fantastic fish, octopuses, whose capacity to give off light achieves near perfection, employing lenses and reflectors and changing color at the animal's wish in order to emit radioactive pulses. This "cold light" is a phenomenon of chemistry and luminescence. Better still, and even more extraordinary: the Prince of Monaco observatory has discovered true phantoms in the seas of the Azores, which only reveal their presence through the movement of water. They possess the organs and systems necessary for life and leave no trace of their passage. But, for me, it is at night that it reaches its apogee. Crustaceans ascend from the deep, covered in their transparent carapace, and the gelatinous creatures that drift immediately under the surface of the water, devouring and being devoured. Along the wide avenues of the ocean float monsters with human crania and hairs that are tentacles, phosphorescent creatures drag themselves through the cemeteries of sludge, and there are octopuses with such powerful suction pads that it is easier to cut off their tentacles than to tear them off. Some of them create blades and hooks on their suction pads that seize and tear or envelop their prey by putting it in a sack. Hatred, carnage, and despair come to the surface sometimes during the mating process; they entwine in death throes, suction pad against suction pad, as if it were necessary to suffer in order to create.

What have I got to do with this life that perturbs and fascinates me? . . . Above all, it is the eyes of these monsters that paralyze me—blue, green, eyes that are extraordinarily fiery, intelligent, and domineering. There are some which are six meters long. Some manage to leave the water and drag themselves along the seashore looking for their prey. If it were not for the whales that contain them within their limits with their insatiable appetite for gelatinous flesh, these monsters would devour the sea and might even dare to devour the land . . .

Deeper still, down in the furthest depths, the feature-
less slime, the slime from which emerge the skeletons of
wrecked ships, machinery buried in the cement-colored sed-
iment, fashioned from all manner of residues and covering
the great depths that we assumed were dead. It is there that
life is generated. The sea is life—but the sea is also the image
of reality or of the inferno, which is all the same thing. Further up, fish with monstrous shapes swim and violent forces
are unleashed. One can glimpse huge, round, toothless
mouths, made to suck, and enormous bellies that need to be
filled. All shapes and sizes: the manta ray, a huge, black, voracious, birdlike creature, spread out like a cloak; the great ray
or common torpedo fish that torments whoever touches it;
the slender blue shark, the cow shark, the extravagant sunfish, with two vertical fins, one sticking upwards, the other
down; the porpoise with its big sharp beak; the blowfish,
which is called a *tamboril,* or monkfish in the Algarve; the
needlefish, with its sword always drawn in its mouth; the
insatiable shark, with its parasitical shark-sucker attached
to its chin by a suction pad; the angular rough shark, that
puffs up when it is taken from the water and which emp-
ties itself in order to dive; the magnificent shoals of small
fish; mackerel that on pristine mornings bubble and boil on
the surface of the water. All of the fishermen tell us of fish,
recounting extraordinary incidents, above all concerning the
merraxo, melraxo, and *rinquim,* which is what they call the
shark on Faial and Pico. A dry, dark-skinned man, a cousin
of the Chatinhas, recounts:

"My brother Manuel went out fishing, and I was in another
boat. Manuel went ahead to get enough fish to fill the basket and came across a shoal of jack mackerel. He started to
use his landing net on them, but there were so many sharks
about that he pulled it out so as not to lose it. He saw all those
open mouths around him and tried to get away, but those

merraxos began to nudge the boat so hard that they almost made it turn turtle. He thought he was done for—their mouths looked ever greedier as they almost leaped aboard. He prodded them with a stick to try and get free of them. The sea was full of *merraxos* . . . Manuel hoisted his flag to request help . . ."

"Where was this?"

"Just outside the Norte fishing ground, off the Salão coast. Whenever there are a lot of jack mackerel, or there's a lot of whale blood, the *merraxos* head for the bait straightaway. Then . . ."

Then he describes a scene that I am unable to reproduce, all about voracious mouths and slippery skins, falling over each other in the sea, leaping out of the sea, a vivid image of hellish greed. Skin and mouths, feverish skin, swishing, slipping, diving, and rising entangled together in the churning water, only mouths and fearsome expressions of greed and rage filling the water.

"I reached him and asked him about the mackerel, and he answered that what he wanted was to get away from those sharks that were chasing the shoal. Then I noticed them and saw so many heads that I didn't dare put my net in. What was happening there in the water was frightening. All you could see on the surface was a mass of seething skin and mouths. A big cow shark arrived and bit the *merraxo*, lifting it up between its teeth. Then an albacore came and butted the boat so hard that Manuel fell into the well and was unable to work for days after . . . We thought we were done for, and the upheaval was so big that boats from São Jorge and Faial rushed to the spot thinking it was a whale . . . Yes, sir, when one or two of those creatures get under the boat, they ruin everything!"

Rays and torpedo fish, of a disproportionate size, also attack boats, and if a man falls overboard, they will wrap him in their viscous cloak and drag him down to the bottom. Desembate tells the story that he was out in a jon boat fishing, and had lowered his anchor, when some fish or other got tangled in the rope and dragged the boat along at top speed, faster than a steamer. He was going to die . . . Another one tells of being caught by a cow shark weighing six or seven tons: its liver alone furnished two barrels of oil. It is a fish that swims at great depths, and can weigh as much as ten tons, while fishermen distinguish between two varieties—the mild cow shark and the wild cow shark. Others have surprised a needlefish and a shark fighting each other. The needlefish is a long, pale-blue creature, with a narrow head, and attacks the monster, which veers off on its side, keeping a close watch on it, and when it senses its proximity, it severs its tail, invariably emerging victorious.

"They were battling each other when we harpooned the needlefish. And then the *merraxo* threw itself at the boat like a fiend . . ."

If there is a living image of the Inferno, it is the sea, where fish devour each other in a struggle to the death—large and small, monsters that await their prey without moving, their eyes white and fixed, and those that are whipped, lacerated, ripped by the tentacles and suction pads of their victims before they can eat them. There are fish that are devoured by parasites; there are others that introduce themselves inside the other and will not let it go before they have eaten it all, leaving only the skin. All manner of fantasies and horrific dramas are possible in the sea, even extending nowadays to the belief in a serpent capable of devouring ships.

Over all this, the flat blue expanse of sky, which makes us avoid thinking about the half-dozen planks between us and disaster. The porpoises leap along in schools, and flying fish flee with their enemies in pursuit; great dark turtles bob along the surface and sometimes, in the distance, one can see the vaporous jets from a whale, as in some primitive picture, and one can find a singular creature that spends its whole life following a wooden plank that has fallen into the sea, as if it were fulfilling its destiny. It never loses it. This creature is the sunfish, accompanied by a shoal of smaller fish, which, when the plank and their guide are taken from the water, prefer to allow themselves to be caught and die rather than abandon it. For them, the plank is their destiny. Their destiny ends in that infinite bitter tragedy . . . When the whalers from Lajes do Pico come across dolphins or *moleiros,* which are bigger than porpoises, with a flat head and a gray body, these offer themselves up in a fatal onrush.

They migrate across the Atlantic and enter the Mediterranean in their hundreds and thousands, always together like brothers and one behind the other. Where one puts its snout, the others follow suit, and if one ends up on the coast, all the others follow to their death.

That water, which swirls around in blue vitreous shards and torrents, blue-green, deep-green, whirling one over the other, that water may after all be a body with a life we do not fully comprehend, sustaining and supporting its creatures in its maternal embrace. A vital water full of minerals that leads and carries them in its seething blueness, without their feeling its weight. The air sustains us, but does not lift us up, it has no variety, while the ocean in its nurturing, is another mother, less fragile, stronger, and more fertile.

"Dolphins ahoy!"

The whole population rushes to the beach in a clamor of excitement. They throw themselves into the boats, making a hell of a racket, or grab stones and tie them to string to splash the water and scare the dolphins, which are very timid creatures. Those out on the sea in the boats gradually hem them in, whistling at them, slowly pushing them towards the coast, until they can encircle them with large nets that are thrown out between the Carreira and Palmeirim rocks. At that point, the shouting and the carnage begin to reverberate. The women on the shore, the people in the boats throw stones at the pod, which cannot get away and becomes completely disorientated, writhing around in the restricted space, showing their spines and their dorsal fins or wildly jerking their tails in the water. The whistling increases—the shouting gets louder. The siege closes in ever more tightly—the butchery is about to begin . . . Women, men, boys wave harpoons and metal-tipped wooden spears, lances, and boathooks. Ah! . . . The dolphins throw themselves in panic against the rocks, after trying to escape out to sea. The surface of the water is already full of thick slicks of blood, among a seething mass of skin and tails in the churning pool.

All around, the excitement grows and the laughter, the shouts coming from gaping mouths—the hubbub, the folk clapping their hands as they climb into the water to kill more effectively. One group casts ropes and pull the creatures nearer. Boys wait on the rocks clutching knives. The dolphins dragged along the coast moan—they moan like men in their death agony. The water is a lake of blood between ornate rocks. Whirlpools of color and gestures, hysterical yells of fury and pleasure, the final death throes in the ever bloodier water.

One or two that manage to escape do not even try to get further away—they return to meet their end next to the dead. The frenzied bloodlust has reached its climax. The party ends as suddenly as it began—the fun is over. The massacre was of no tangible value. At the most, they use the oil from these creatures melted down as fuel for their lamps.

Hidden corners, holes, cavities, and caves seethe with life. The Enxaréus cave, on Flores, opens its gaping black mouth onto the sea. Rocky, a dark dome, streaked with white and crisscrossed with black ridges. It bears above it the weight of

a whole mountain; down below, in the deep blue water, swim
thousands of black-tailed trevallies. In this sheltered spot one
sometimes finds more fish than water, making it an almost
compact mass. In this dramatically rocky cavern, which looks
like the entrance to Dante's Inferno, voices reverberate in a
chilling echo. In the Boqueirão cave on the same island, with
its corroded gray rock veering to green at its base, the water
forms a deep pool, and one can watch fish as if in an aquar-
ium, shadows that glimmer and disappear among floating
golden weed in the rise and fall of the waves. There are thousands of small fish the color of old copper: the wrasse, the
croaker, and the scorpionfish, which is red all over; the grunt,
and other bigger ones with lighter bellies. Next to the jagged
cliff faces, the blue is as dark as writing ink. I spend hours
lying on the rock contemplating the crystalline water, from
where pieces of red clay emerge, reflecting the movement of
the blue waters. On other rocks, at Caveira, for example, one
finds barnacles, moss-covered stones (among which shellfish
live), shapeless pebbles inhabited by a worm that has a delicate taste of the sea. On Corvo, there are *mouras,* black crabs
the color of black rock, and, at the foot of the remains of
the formless, mutilated statue facing towards America, hundreds of sharks tangle with each other, showing their white
bellies. If one is in a boat, one may see a black bream with its
coppery colors glinting in the depths, and ghostly shadows
passing this way and that, while successive waves roll in over
the surface of the water.

In thousands of places on Pico, water flows in and is
trapped in pools. Outside, the rumble of the waves makes
us feel sleepy. There is no one: just water in the pools, so
clear that one can make out the bottom, light and translu-
cent as the air and, down there, shoals of little fish, prickly
and with beaks, and others that look like flocks of birds. On
the Princesa Alice bank, thirty miles from Varadouro, where

the depth is twenty fathoms, shallow by comparison to the great deeps of the Azorean seas, there is an abundance of forkbeards and congers, and all the fish that do not dwell in the deepest waters.

I feel like making the boat my home, traveling ports and roadsteads, living in permanent contact with this inexhaustible, fecund life. Finding a good anchorage, going ashore only to get water. And never to stop again! Never! To live! Live in the open air, drop anchor in the lee of a rock emerging all red from the water—a red that glitters in the blue waters—or discover a tavern in some little harbor with half a dozen dwellings, where they know the secret of a good fish stew or how to prepare those tasty barnacles that smell and taste of the sea! I would sleep when the sea is calm and the sails slacken, under a shower of stars pricking the water and lulled as if in my mother's lap!

The sun rises. High up in the atmosphere, the fragility, the beauty, the joy of the birds, of the gulls, which the boys on Flores call *passarocas*, throwing stones at them when they screech—skaah! skaah! . . .

> Mad old passaroca,
> Your father died
> Your grandma came a cropper! . . .

The shearwaters chatter all night and spend the day floating on the sea in huge flocks, over a shoal of jack mackerel. The delicate tern, gray and white with a black head, which arrives in spring and migrates to Africa in October and November, and the lesser tern, which likes storms and appears in winter, fill the air with their fluttering and life with their magic. It is on the rocks off Madalena that the terns come to breed, fly, and live. There are two large red rocks in the middle of the sea—the flat islet and the tall islet. This is where they have their nests and from where they take off in extraordinary wheeling flights, filling the world with their plumage. These dainty birds, after rearing their young, when the weather is still good, but sensing the approach of winter, assemble in flocks that come from the rocks and from the other islands, and all together take off in search of more favorable climes. If one is left behind, it dies. But among all these varieties, there is one little bird that interested and attracted me in particular. Leaning on the stern rail of the ship, I saw them, not much larger than swallows, black with a white spot near the tail, swooping backwards and forwards in flocks over the whitened, foamy water churned up by the propeller, diving, wheeling, returning to the swirling sea. And all the time, this was happening under the power of their wings on the high seas, far from land. These are the black-and-white shearwaters, which never abandon the wake of the ship, searching for food in the seething water and accompanying the ship to the remotest parts of the Atlantic. The sailors, who never see them land and, when they look, always see them flying in the ship's wake, say that they build their nest under their wing. This frenzy, this beating of wings, this dauntless fragility in the vast solitude of the ocean instilled in me an impression of life and matchless vigor, as if I were watching these creatures, born and raised on the sea, emerging from its belly.

Vision of Madeira

August 13

I have never forgotten that pristine Madeira morning, and the colors that ranged from gray to gold, from gold to indigo—nor the yawning mountain before me, streaming with blue and green . . .

I get up while on board, in search of light—another light of the type into which I was born and raised, and which I am beginning to yearn for ever more strongly. I am anxious to see it again, that cloudless blue, that pure, golden, vivid light. But the day is still overcast: the same clouds, possibly a little lighter, in delicate brushstrokes and, on the pale sea, the little streaks of white horses bob on the surface. Four in the afternoon: I sense out there, in the background, over the undulations of the waves, a strip of another blue—the blue that one might breathe. As if bidding me farewell, light rain showers

fall. Back in the direction of the Azores, darker clouds continue to amass: they are all blowing, attracted to the islands,
as if they had a destiny to fulfill . . .

Early evening and a blue, indistinct mass starts to rise up
in front of me, with a gray cloud crouching over it. The sun,
shining on its topmost parts, illuminates the cone of a mountain and floods out between patches of mist over the extrem-
ities of an almost pitch-black hillside. By now, one can make
out the distorted jaggedness of the land and the cliff faces,
wrapped in vapors that billow into the open crevices in the
rock; they stand out majestically against the lead-gray horizon. The harshness, the rocky plateaus, the ravines are all
accentuated, along with the ferrous, perpendicular gashes;
one can imagine the drama of its birth, full of convulsions
and earth-slips, when the great cataclysm ripped through and
dismembered the submerged continent, leaving behind open
sores from its remains, which still shed blood today. And
on the patches of sooty ash, that fell willy-nilly and spread
towards the seashore, there clung half a dozen little cottages,
having as their background the thick mass of rock thrown up
behind them. It is six o'clock: everything moves forward and
imposes itself in purple, with green strips of crops and gilded
crests of mountains; to the north, there is an agglomeration
of grim rocky stacks that conceal the earth.

And the coast advances straight towards me, all the time
more forbidding and dark. It instills fear. One can hardly
distinguish the forests on the mist-covered heights, and the
deep valleys down which water must rush in torrents during
winter. The ship follows the coast, which, on this side of
the island, has no backdrop, revealing to us the Madeira
that appears to have been cut with an axe from end to end,
throwing the other half into the sea. It is a harsh, dramatic
bronze, which contrasts with the approach to Funchal and
the island's other coast. I stand looking at the villages as

they pass—Jardim do Mar, Paul do Mar, clinging to the cliffs, where all I can see in detail are volcanic excoriations with their patina of verdigris. Only man! Only man has the effrontery to cultivate terraces opened up with fire on the perpendicular cliff face! (We are sailing so close to land that I can hear roosters crowing.) Madalena do Mar hemmed in by two cliffs whose dark shapes are reflected in the velvet waters. Ponta do Sol and Cabo Girão, which the night makes denser and more massive . . . All this panorama in the gray twilight assumes extraordinary proportions, its black outline against the leaden sky, transformed by the cloud flying ever lower, and unfolding in further contours over the still, inky waters. By now, I can hardly make out the huge Cruz headland, behind which our port of arrival awaits us. At each moment that passes, the cliff face that stands between us and the world appears ever higher and darker to me. There is only a vague flicker of light on the seaward side; the rest is a sheer, vast blackness in league with the dense mist and the impalpability of the night. A tiny speck of light appears in this vast solitude and in the ever-thicker mass. It is a sign of subversive human presence, one man, doubly isolated between the mountain and the sea. It is one soul. And that tiny humble light, for me, becomes resplendent in its grandeur: it is a star that causes me to meditate.

August 14

In the morning, I wake up ashore. I open the window and a smell of truffles wafts in. I go out and explore immediately— the back lanes full of life, the little streets cobbled with greasy pebbles, where oxcarts without wheels slide by, painted yellow, with fresh clean awnings and curtains made of leafy branches open in the middle. I gaze at the yellow and white houses, with their red gables and green shutters, which give

Funchal its intimate, familiar character. Everything takes
me by surprise: the heat, the strong light, the garden with
ferns and a huge jacaranda with purple blossom, trees permeated with contentment, which in the stillness and silence
gradually shed their flowers on the ground, leaving a crimson puddle all around. A drop of water falls over there in
the background into a static pool of more water. The air
is heady with scent. I sit down under the huge plane trees
which greet us as we come ashore—a delightful, impenetrable mass. I climb: an irregular square and then the church,
a great sandalwood box with gilded curlicues and mother-
of-pearl incrustations. Inside, it smells of incense and pre-
cious wood; outside, above the tiled roofs, one never loses
sight of the rough, bare outline of the mountains. I head
for the market—the market attracts me: it is tiny, with two
or three trees and a fountain, and it brims with fruit like a
full basket—bunches of yellow bananas, two-handled *alcofa*
baskets overflowing with apricots, ripe black figs, half-open
and oozing with juice. All of the fruit here is delicious, and
the banana leaves a persistent perfume in your mouth forever afterwards. To the sound of the marble fountain, which
glimmers with its threads of water and topped with its Leda
hugging her voluptuous swan, this goes to make up a little
gouache picture, with abundant sunlight overhead. At first
sight, it is confusing: one has to step back in order to contemplate it, as if one were doing a painted sketch, to make
out the golden grapes, papayas, the red of the tomatoes, the
caged macaws and exotic birds hanging from the branches
of the trees, and, under the awnings, between the squeals of
monkeys from São Tomé and the singing speech of the people of Madeira, the women with white scarves round their
heads and tall gumboots and shawls, who are preparing food
for the Monte festival, the men, gaunt and dark-skinned, the
short-haired English women, with their white dresses cut to

the same pattern that England manufactures and exports to the whole world. One's vision is disturbed and falters, the smell is intoxicating. You need to put your paintbrush to work to bring out those backgrounds of purple shadows with a lot of blue, the deep green of the cabbages, and the dizzying picture of the water-speckled fountain. See how the very shadow is luminous and pulsating. And, along with it, the gold of the bananas palpitates, along with the yellow of the melons, and the intense red of the chili peppers tied together in bundles. And if a basket is removed from the shade into the light, the fruits sparkle, burn, and acquire extraordinary transparency. And all the time, the water drips, refreshing the picture, mixed with the glint of sunlight, which filters here and there through the trees in the slightest of brushstrokes.

But to see the city and its suburbs together, one must climb up to the Pico de Barcelos. As I leave the center, small isolated houses begin to appear amidst gardens, and the large leaves of banana trees, still in deep red bud or from where there hangs the already ripened fruit. When one eventually reaches the top, the whole majestic amphitheater lies before us. It is a great shell, bounded on one side by the Pico do Garajau and on the other by the Ponta de Santa Cruz, with the undulating mountain behind. The valleys and their contour lines originate high above, torn open by torrents of water over a bed of chipped stones that are blue and slippery. All of this is dark, leaden, because the sky is lined with clouds that envelop the hills.

To appreciate the whole scene, one needs to choose the morning, the evening, or the clear winter days, because the sky over Madeira is always cloudy; the mists billow down the vast barrier that occupies the entire skyline on the landward side, and descend as far as the sea down a slope quilted with crops and dotted with houses that get nearer and nearer to each other, packed together by the time we reach the alluring

white city. Everything one can see, with the exception of
the jagged peaks, has been divided into fruit and vegetable
gardens, into terraces of lush green cane, little gardens left
in their natural state, where clumps of banana trees have
sprouted, all in a profusion that dazzles and astonishes one.
There are miles of fertile land, gardens, fields, and crops that
leave us humble and dumbstruck. On my right, the range of
hills extends as far as Câmara dos Lobos. Only after I have
become used to all this—my eyes were wallowing in the
blue—am I able to distinguish the violet streaks of the slopes,
the country houses high up amid vines and orchards, the rustic buildings hanging on the rock faces and clinging to the
mountain, which has been cut in half by a violent, dramatic
gash. I am busy trying to pin down the character of this landscape . . . It attracts all our senses and only has one desire—to
mollify us while at the same time throwing us off balance . . . I
peer at the gardens of the manor houses, where everything is
kept aligned and correct, and the rustic cottages, which I find
heartwarming. As I pass by, my eye catches an embankment.
Sometimes a whitewashed wall with half a dozen pots of
flowers is enough for me to feel a sensation of enchantment
that I do not find here. What is missing is a little touch of melancholy, that spirit of certain little nooks one finds in Portugal, where a couple of little fields, a church, a cluster of pines,
and some rustling grass fill us with a delicious sensation of
repose and gentle nostalgia. I miss the pale, misty mornings,
the golden woebegone days with one or two blemishes. This
landscape is not happy with two or three trees, a refined air,
and pallid watery blue: it is heavy and demanding. It is carnal
and dissolute. At the same time, it is beautiful.

Words convey little in such cases: the main thing about
Madeira is that the light creates and ripens the vista as much
as it does the fruit, because the only image I can find for everything is that of a ripe fruit that has gradually, like someone

who has nothing else to do, taken on the colors of the sun, in the morning and at sunset, and has attained a perfect state that simultaneously delights and permeates the air with perfume. The land emerges from the inky sea with the warm tones of pineapple, which is the strawberry of the tropics—paradise without cold or heat, to which one can add the taste of wines taken in sips, and whose transparency is appreciated by holding the glass up to the light. The light! To be able to reproduce it, that would be everything, but only a painter can discover this golden light—diluted blue that envelops this whole landscape lying at our feet like a woman offering her firm breasts with brazenness and innocence at the same time. The very trees that burst out on all sides are made of flesh—the strange tropical vegetation mixed up with all the others: cypresses, cacti, glossy plants, amid clusters of humble pines and huge, strong, immobile creatures spreading their branches over the streets. At school, I learned that time-honored story about the three kingdoms of Nature—but here, the trees, which are so vigorous and of such abundant foliage, belong, without a shadow of doubt, to the animal kingdom.

August 15

I have been unable to get to sleep these last few nights. Two, three hours without sleeping. In the street, serenades with guitars and automobiles rolling by with women in them. Night is voluptuous and the air of this tropical climate a caress the moment the sun goes down. In the morning I head for the mountains.

From Funchal southwards, the coast is almost all sheer: Santa Cruz, and up there on top of it, the Senhor da Serra; a huge gulch into which the sea flows—Machico, and then straight after Caniçal, just up the coast, and the whimsical outline of the Ponta de São Lourenço. Beyond this cape, the north coast begins, the wildest, greenest, and possibly the most beautiful part of this island which is so diverse and ornate. In the early evening those hillsides, so formidable when seen from the ship, form a dense backdrop unrolling in dark patches, with the last rays of sunlight clinging on to that vast mass, which seems all the more immense at this hour. Madeira is a range of mountains that fall away suddenly on the west coast, descending to the sea on the north coast, and with the more cultivated land in the valleys and gulches, which are flooded by streams of water.

The interior of the island is bare mountain, with the exception of Paul da Serra. The best, most sheltered area for agriculture, where snow, which they call *folheto* here, never falls, is the south, where sugarcane is cultivated on the coast, and vines on the slopes. Curral das Freiras—in the central cordillera, is a strange valley produced by an eruption, a huge ravine squeezed between almost sheer escarpments, with fearsome depths that reach eight hundred meters, and here one comes across little lost villages such as Livramento, Fajã Escura, Curral, etc. This convulsed, lacerated place may explain the island's formation, for it is here that one finds the most vestiges of craters, with evidence of relatively recent eruptions, in the pools of Porto Moniz, Caniça, Caniçal, etc.

The narrow ravines pass before my eyes, by now bathed in shadow, with only one slope fully lit up, deep, vertical cliff faces—rocky summits thrown up by the eruption, the stream that flows at the base of the Ruivo and Canário mountains— little villages that are so isolated high on the side of the mountain—Pico da Figueira, Curral, Fajã Escura—gullies forming the beds for rushing torrents—isolated, stony lands, where the devil must walk on days when the wind is strong.

Then the landscape changes again: the mountains resemble wild, ruined castles from medieval times. The vegetation is different—bay and lime trees in the hollows, where humidity is greatest. Desolation and surprise, contrasts, ample views of both mountains and sea, such as at the top of the Senhor da Serra, where one's lungs are too small to breathe in the atmosphere of the place and its fragrance. Now we come to a gloomy spot, Câmara dos Lobos, between blackened cliffs, and reeking of fish, then some hamlets next to little cultivated plots, with bundles of firewood drying outside the doors of the humble cottages. Sometimes there is a little dam for preserving water for irrigation, the cleft through which the water flows, down below the abyss, with a huge ridge jutting out next to it, which fills the place with shadow and terror: there are places like this in Curral, which only benefit from five or six hours of sunlight per day.

I set off along the roads and tracks at first light or in the evening, when the sun is sinking behind the mountains, bathing them in a halo. I discover sudden little corners, the blackened village houses, rural and maritime life and their various cultural traditions, for in Madeira all possible climates exist, from the cold north to the heat of the tropics—and I collect a variety of little tableaus which alone would go to form one compact book . . .

There are only two ways to travel in the interior of Madeira in any degree of comfort—in a hammock suspended on a stick carried on the backs of two men who walk carrying wooden staffs, or in an oxcart. But the hammock makes you fall asleep, which is why the cart is preferable. It is set on wooden boards or sleds, called *cursões*. This pretty method of transport has two wicker chairs padded with cloth, decorated

with a blue flowery pattern, and is protected from the sun by
an awning with curtains. A man walks alongside, carrying a
cattle prod, and talks to the oxen, while a little cowherd boy
walks in front. This is the most original way to travel along
the streets and roads, and at the same time it is the fastest,
because the oxen trot and even gallop when necessary. Without the brutality and impersonality of machinery, or the silly
speed of the automobile, this little Funchal cart allows us to
notice things and make remarks while giving the impression
that it is floating and that we have returned to a primitive,
heroic age—it is both a cart and a boat.

Off we go up the cobbled road, between towering chestnut trees. The chestnut is a prodigious tree. Every time I
come across one, I tremble and pause. Chestnuts and running water, water that gushes and meets us on its way down
the road, and never leaves us until we reach the top, watering each farmstead, distributed along channels—water that
comes from the mountains and greets each house every
morning: "hello, hello, hello!" It speaks to all the trees and
gives new vigor to the exhausted flowers. The delicate fronds
of the chestnuts and palms wave in the breeze. There is such
a strong smell of fruit that I peer into the impenetrable little
farmsteads: all I can see are colorful patches of flowers and
groves of greengage trees, soaked and ripened by the sun.
A wall on either side. And this is not enough: shutters make
these solitary dwellings even more jealously guarded and
poetic. What is happening inside? Some torrid love story or
some great dream? Whoever built these did so in order to
live cut off from the world with a woman and sensuous plea-
sures, behind the walls of sumptuous farms, where verdure
overflows, even in the most humble dwellings, which are as
grand as palaces. From here and elsewhere one is blessed with
the extraordinary spectacle of mountains and sea, in a scene
of luxury and voluptuousness. It is a vista that reminds one

of human flesh; it is a panorama, an Eden of wantonness that invades our eyes and our sense of smell at the same time. The low branches, weighed down by their clusters of fruit, offer us golden canvases, the slim leaves of cane over the earthen furrows, the banana tree proffering us its ripe bunches in the strong, bright sun. Up above, we feel like lying down under the trees, venturing into the still slumbering farms, stretching out in all the verdant nooks where leaves rustle in the tepid air, the magical air that I inhale impatiently and where the perfume of fruit, the tang of the sea, the soul of the plants, and a silence replete with life all mingle together.

"Yaah! Yaah!"

The sled slips over the cobblestones. The boy walks in front of the oxen with a fly whisk in his hand, and a man who talks to the creatures walks alongside:

"Yaah! Yaah!"

He does not prod them, nor is there any need: with incredible care, placing their feet and tautening their muscles, they gradually climb each stage of the steep lane, which is the way to reach Monte. From time to time, the boy places a roll of waxed cloth under the sled, for the old cart's boards to slide more smoothly.

"Yaah! Yaah!"

The Fonte square is an expanse of ground with half a dozen huge plane trees filling this place suspended between sky and sea with grandeur, freshness, and shade, with the Bom Jesus church at one end and along the sides the palatial buildings of the sanatorium. These trees alone are worth an empire. For the moment, I do not want to look back . . . We enter a more forbidding region, darkened by pine trees, and I begin to notice the people passing us at this early morning hour . . . Already, at first light, English women come sliding down the lane at full speed inside the wicker basket that the man guides, pushes, or stops by maneuvering his feet. An old

lady passes by carrying chickens for market on the sled, boys
with bundles of firewood and farmers using the same method
of transport to carry logs. Among the figures in this moving
picture, I notice an ancient couple, she wrinkled and ugly
with an old patched shawl, he wizened, a tasseled bonnet on
his head with ear flaps for winter, both of them solemn and
absorbed, as if they were on their way to fulfill a mission.
They are of another age, and I am moved by them. Later,
further along the cobbled lane, amidst the noise of running
water—water is always flowing along the gullies by the side
of the narrow thoroughfare—I encounter women carrying
loads on their head and clutching wooden staffs, young boys
with baskets of sweet or seed potatoes, milkmen with curved
shoulder poles, at either end of which hang two pails . . .

I reach Terreiro da Luta and, at this point, I turn round.
The first impression is only of light, golden light and the
green mountain emerging from the violet sea. Just a few
hues and ecstasy. Not a cloud, not an atom of haze. A youth-
ful, delicate light, an atmosphere to fill our lungs, and at the
same time a heady touch of purity and sensuality to contemplate with apprehension and tenderness. This morning is a
delicious moment in life, before a perfect assemblage freshly
fashioned by the hand of God and floating in the ether. It
is vast and yet it is nothing: it is a world, and it is a hanging
droplet of water reflecting the light of the universe, which
lasts for a second and then falls for ever. The island, with its
tropical verdure, emerges from the violet sea, and there in
the background is Funchal, all white, awakening and stretching itself, still dizzy with sleep . . .

We continue towards Arrebentão and then later to Poiso,
a habitual stop for morning coffee for anyone traveling to

Ribeiro Frio. On the way there, one crosses hill after rounded, ochre-colored hill, with bluish stones breaking through their sunbaked skin, along a road where only the *tabaibeira,* or barbary fig tree, extends its open-palmed hands at the passersby. A stop in the open space by the inn for men and animals to take a rest, and then we begin our descent through increasing solitude until the steep track, where the oxen serve as a brake for the little cart without wheels, as if they were descending the sheer face of the Clérigos Tower.[20] Once again, greenery breaks out in great cascades everywhere, oak trees, beech, chestnut, and I come across my beloved water in a *levada,* which cools and refreshes us throughout the journey. The most rugged gullies, huge gulches that look as if they are on the point of losing their balance and tumbling into the dried-up watercourse, the stones of which glimmer like glass. Trees in an abundance of green thrown together to form a bridge or scattered willy-nilly down the slope, a vegetation that clings as well as it can to the vast cliff face—and down there at the bottom, lost in the wilderness, a hamlet of half a dozen thatched houses that resemble beehives. The only sound that reaches us is that of the smithy's anvil. It is another kind of nature at its wildest that has nothing to do with the tropics: these are features of the northern side of the island . . . The fog surprises whoever comes from above, from splendid sunshine, as it thickens and clears allowing one to suddenly distinguish fantastic details, lush wooded spots, and lone rocks. It wafts up or billows down, enveloping everything, making the landscape more distant to our eyes, and it seems to have been brought in especially to transform it into something still more phantasmagorical. We continue

---

[20] The tower of the eighteenth-century Clérigos church in Oporto is one of the landmarks of Brandão's native city (translator's note).

our downward journey, and the *levada* accompanies us along the sheer cliff face.

That place lost at the bottom is Ribeira da Ametade, the village that can barely be distinguished, Faial, and a huge jagged rock in front of me, known as the Mirante. I pause, awestruck before these scenes, one after the other, rising into the air and dissolving, the narrow valleys that seem even more isolated and compact, even deeper, protected and crushed by fearsome rocks, and through which torrents must flow with an angry roar during winter. Is it reality or mist? . . . These are landscapes by Doré—places at once tormented, untamed, and poetic. A chaos with some lyrical touches. And the water always follows us, while the fog distorts everything, gray, almost pink when pierced by the sun, or dense when it infiltrates the gullies, wafting up the mountainsides, gathering in thick smudges, while suddenly thinning to reveal details of the wild, grandiose landscape. I pass through a narrow fissure in the rock (and the water comes through as well); I catch sight of a colossal, perpendicular cliff, and stop in front of the widening valley and the magic of the mist, which creates before me an unruly row of hills tumbling by leaps and bounds into the abyss, with beech trees miraculously clinging to clumps of earth. Near me, the trees are so old that they have beards, lichen beards of a type I have never seen before except on goats. I can now, with some difficulty, make out what is happening. Next to me, there is a huge, imposing boulder, covered in vitreous gray moss, which no doubt will soon move, and, at my feet, the open chasm, all shrouded in mist . . . A truly thick mist, from which there suddenly bursts a ghostly outcrop, slender, dark, fierce, coming straight at me. I think I catch a glimpse of the sea through a crack—a little bridge—a hut—a drop of water falling from the mountains between smooth stones, until the fog at last moves and spreads definitively, confusing and enveloping everything.

Only the babble of the *levada* persists beside me, summoning me back to a sense of reality.

We return; the track climbs, the boy shouts, "Yaah! Yaah!" until we reach the sunlit region again. The light is not chaste as it is in the Azores, nor the mountains green. The tones are warm, the hilltops parched, and the mist lingers deep down on the valley floors. Bands of crickets jump from the remains of the grass already burnt up by the sun, but that still smell good. All the way to Monte there are the same rounded hollows, where clumps of heather grow, and here and there a thicket of jimsonweed. The pinewoods make the journey monotonous until we arrive back at Monte once more. The moment we arrive, I stop in front of a solitary little house in the forest. It is a single-story abode, with little sash windows overlooking the sea. It is worthless: it is no more than a snail's abandoned shell. But it does not look as if it were ever built; it looks as if it grew at the same time as the red flowers surrounding it and that remind us of some great passion or crime. Trees, four old walls around it, a vine trained along wooden poles at the entrance to the garden, and a magical quality that is hard to explain and which is born from simple things that do not seek to grab our attention, but only offer us their warmth. This is an ideal spot to spend one's final days ignored, one's eyes fixed on the sea and warmed in winter by this splendid sun, plunging my frigid old age into this radiant light and stretching out my weary body in the shade of trees that offer us their fruits. I would have a whitewashed trough with pots of flowers that no one grows anymore, but that my grandmother cultivated in a flowerbed—dahlias, morning glories, geraniums. I would seek refuge in that shady corner where there is a trickle of water amid half a dozen banana trees, that I can never look at without being astonished. They live cozily together in this sheltered spot, the dwarf much shorter, the gold and silver one, whose trunk grows

much taller, and which has a plume of decorative leaves at
the top, reminiscent of a scene from *Paul et Virginie*. Some
have dangling bunches, others a great bleeding bud—leaves
in overlapping layers, with a faded yellow flower hidden
inside. Apart from being beautiful, they are prolific. They
produce their fruit throughout the year, then die, but new
shoots follow. They are prodigious in their fertility. Once the
fruit has ripened, some people cut the whole bunch off with
the adjoining branch, and carry it home on their back . . . I
notice down at the bottom of the abyss a cavern of inter-
twined arms—half a dozen square meters of primeval forest; I notice dark paths between dense rows of bamboo and,
among the dried grass, seed heads that one feels like picking
as if they were coins. It was here that Daudet should have
installed his teacher of idleness, who lay in the shade of a
garden in Algiers, waiting for figs to fall into his mouth . . . To
put it more precisely: this place is for meditators to live and
die. Above all to live, for the great delight of a climate such
as this is to live and breathe its sensuous air. To the balsam
of this land's atmosphere, one should add the violet breath
of the sea. One can sleep in the open air under the canopy of
stars, for the sultry nights of Madeira are like a soft-skinned
caress. There is a scent of flowers and fruit during its clear,
languid nights, nights that shed their petals before our very
gaze, like a camellia slowly dying. Up above, the sky cannot
withstand the weight of the stars, while down below, the city,
full of dots of light, resembles some wondrous constellation.
These humid, moonlit nights, along with having a beloved
woman by our side, are the most extraordinary things it is
possible to have in the world, for the outer voluptuousness
chimes with our inner exaltation, and the universe pulsates
within us until we ache.

I ponder and look. There is an orange tone, turning to
green and blue out to sea, which I shall never see again and

which will never be repeated. There are threads of gold hanging over this scene of nature, which may be unique. I contemplate the little house, the trees—my dream—and I desire nothing more. This is complete and perfect . . . but little by little, I feel a nostalgic yearning . . . It is still almost nothing, I stress. It gathers shape and fills out—a yearning for my big old hearth, blackened by the flames; a yearning for the cold, a yearning that grows stronger and leaves me flustered to my very core. I remember the little farmhouse, its ragged vine shaken by the gales. And this mingles with the splendor of a golden sunset beyond the mountains, which leaves the mountainside all green as it soars upwards into the sky from the violet sea. A fine dust—it is the dying light— floats upwards, nature is bathed in absolute calm . . . What peace! . . . But I am restless and I feel my yearning ever stronger and deeper—yearning for the last evenings in autumn, the first shivers from the chill, the first fires lit, when the hearth's crickets approach the warmth of the flames, as I do, and burst into song all night long. I yearn for the winter.

August 24

Now, I am better acquainted with Madeira. After my initial enthusiasm, I see things in the cold light of day. This island is a spectacle and little else—a dazzling spectacle with aspirations to a life devoid of reality and an absolute scorn for anything that does not have the whiff of being English. Shop signs in English, signposts in English, and everything prepared and planned with precision for the English to see and open their purse strings. They come ashore from ocean liners—and, straightaway, Funchal becomes a theater—they are cold, severe, domineering; the women emerge from the sea dressed like brides, walking stick in hand and crochet blouses, flaunting their self-importance and their pounds

sterling in their conquered land. The English are possibly the
most upstanding people in the world—but they have no sense
of the grotesque. Sitting by the door of the Golden Gate,[21] I
hear the ship's siren, and I already know what is about to
happen: the scene changes as if in some conjurer's trick. Men
with big straw hats appear in order to sell needlework, spoof
coral necklaces, baskets of fruit; the shops are lit up all of a
sudden, and a parade of different types begins—black Cape
Verdean women with red foulard scarves on their head, cor-
pulent women, massive Germans, sickly febrile Portuguese
returning from the colonies, awful old English ladies who
have come from goodness knows where and are going to
goodness knows where, disappearing forever in the fathom-
less mystery of the sea; unbelievable creatures who roll by
at full speed in automobiles, in a momentary frenzy, and all
this happens in the one street where there is a café overflowing with light. But the ship blasts its signal, and an hour later
this fictitious world has disappeared and everything returns
to silence and isolation. The lights are switched off, the shop
window blinds are pulled down, and the hawkers settle back
into their narrow daily routine. The scene is ever-changing
with the arrival and departure of the great ocean liners.

Madeira, however, is also a place to spend the winter, with
one or two magnificent hotels. This almost tropical land,
where the summer heat is moderated by the breeze, except for
days when the sirocco is blowing, when it becomes difficult to
breathe, is a delight in winter. The air is mild, the temperature
warm. Imagine what it must be like to come from London,
the blustery squalls, the freezing cold, the gloominess that
fills you with anxiety and your soul with sadness and apathy,
and, after two days on a steamship, you arrive before this sensuous jewel floating suspended in the azure . . . The port is

---

[21] The name of a well-known café in downtown Funchal (translator's note).

breathtaking. The delicate air one breathes has the scent of fruit—a temperature of twelve degrees and golden sunlight cascading down. Some days are so beautiful one is frightened of touching them—so perfectly still and of a captivating blue. Life has no substance to it, everything is dreamlike. The nights are magical. There are roses everywhere. A warm breeze comes from the mountains. And one savors this, slowly, little by little—it permeates the pores of one's skin and renders our soul languorous. Who can believe in death, horrible, eternal cold, before nature that offers us armfuls of flowers and their scent in the middle of winter? . . . This is when the consumptive are able to breathe . . . "Life!" . . . Women lose their head and drink the amber-colored wine, their mouths half-open like ripe fruit about to fall from the tree. Behind the city, Monte rises skywards, open to the spirit of the place and hardened in its carnality. At night, the frenzy begins. In the large hotels, in their white, low-neckline dresses, inebriated by the music and with that magnificent view before them, they rise from the table and dance cheek to cheek. On the last night of the year, all the houses are illuminated by Bengal flares, crowning this celebration of the wealthy and the foreigners.

Let us now look at the reality behind all this . . . Tourism, alcohol, and sugar have degraded the people and enriched one or two lucky locals. Some men in Funchal, through contact with progress, have turned into hoteliers, shoeshiners, or chauffeurs.

But what about the common people? The degenerate, malnourished men who pass me every day on the street? I contrast the men in Madeira and those of the Azores, the inhabitant of Corvo, for example, isolated from the world and living the same as he has for three centuries, and I ask myself what the city dweller or the peasant has gained from civilization. The traders and hotel owners have profited, but all the rest have sunken into an ever-increasing abject poverty. There is an ever-widening gap between the so-called higher classes and the rest. What is happening in this country is a crime for which we will pay dearly.

The peasant, who in the old days lived on corn pap three times a day and slept happily with his whole family in some hole in the ground, is now an inveterate alcoholic, who has even lost the habit of laughing—(the pilgrimage to Monte is a gloomy occasion). One constantly hears folk say, "He's given in to grog! He's not got any work." Sugarcane is the easiest of all crops to cultivate. After planting, all it needs is to be fertilized and cut regularly for years on end. In the least sheltered part of the island, where the farmer lives poor and isolated, growing corn and making charcoal to sell in the city, some pristine customs are preserved, although these are slowly disappearing. Women embroider. It is the great female industry in both the Azores and Madeira. In almost all the little hovels, one sees young girls busy with their thread, thimble on their finger. America takes everything they produce. The trader provides them with the printed cloth, and they buy the thread. They earn very little. But habits of work are created. They become careful and focused. Once they start to embroider, they talk more quietly. The worst thing is that these women, who are almost all devoid of any grace and who have exchanged their old forms of dress for a mantilla over their head, now join their menfolk in drinking grog and give their children dummies soaked in alcohol.

I know fishermen from Paul, Câmara de Lobos, and Machico. There is no sea more fertile than this. There are times during the year when a vast, dense shoal of skipjacks, a variety of tuna, pass through these waters. The black scabbard fish abounds, along with huge squid, mackerel, yellow-speckled moray eels, but they limit themselves to catching swordfish, which is the easiest, having lost their memory of the seas and their fish: "Only Patudo knew them all, and only Andorico goes for bass, because he knows where to find them." "He drinks all he earns—he drinks everything." They drink local and foreign liquor. In Funchal, there are taverns wherever you look. There are places at the back of clothes shops, with English women sipping their drinks. Goldsmiths are simultaneously goldsmiths and tavern keepers; dressmakers have a counter and a row of glasses . . . At the entrance to the port, there is one on each side, with barrels ready to dispense drink . . . This is a far cry from those simple people, those stout men I said farewell to with a heavy heart . . .

When it comes to it, between tourism, which has produced such results, and hospitality, I have no hesitation in saying that I detest tourism and love hospitality. I love the old Spain, for so long resistant to exploitation, refusing to adapt to the wishes of foreigners and to satisfy them with a false smile to the point of changing their habits and customs for the sake of appearing nice. The foreigner inevitably arrives in a tourist country as he does a hotel—as the one who is paying. Now a nation should not be a hotel—and God save us from having to be one! And if the rich could only remember that there are thousands of impoverished children in Lisbon, while, up there, there are one or two German mansions that are empty and left to rot away over time! . . . While on this subject, I would like to register this plea for compassion: when I saw those huge deserted hotels, I remembered the consumptive children of the Alfama and Mouraria. I think the government and the wealthy could well take them into their care, sending them for a few months to this admirable climate bathed in light and sunshine. It could represent salvation for many of them. The great hotels, with tail-coated waiters, music, and flowers, could pay for these wretched abandoned creatures dying of hunger and poverty, providing them with shelter and care. And perhaps saving them . . .

August 29

I am beginning to feel restless. I have not been able to sleep: all night long, I have fervently yearned for another light—the light in which I was reared. Not even the light of Madeira satisfies me. It tires me. Every morning, I peer at the clouded sky waiting for the light to break through. I board the ship. I spend the night of 29 August on deck, all the time waiting anxiously for the light—and the whole night is dark and stormy. On deck, all I can see is the pitch-blackness stirred by clamor. But in the morning, the squall has passed by the time we enter Cascais Bay—and the light bursts through, a joyous light, a light that makes everything vibrant, a light in which each atom has wings and comes directly towards me like an arrow of gold. In the vast blue freedom of the sky, the sun floats as if in some great fluid mass. Portugal! . . .